Helping Children Manage Stress
A Guide for Adults

James H. Humphrey

Foreword by Paul J. Rosch
President, The American Institute of Stress

Child & Family Press   •   Washington, DC

Child & Family Press is an imprint of the Child Welfare League of America. The Child Welfare League of America (CWLA) is a privately supported, nonprofit, membership-based organization committed to preserving, protecting, and promoting the well-being of all children and their families. Believing that children are our most valuable resource, CWLA, through its membership, advocates for high standards, sound public policies, and quality services for children in need and their families.

CHILD WELFARE LEAGUE OF AMERICA, INC.
440 First Street, NW, Third Floor, Washington, DC 20001-2085
E-mail: books@cwla.org

CURRENT PRINTING (last digit)
10 9 8 7 6 5 4 3 2 1

Cover design by Veronica J. Morrison

Printed in the United States of America

ISBN # 0–87868-668-1

Library of Congress Cataloging-in-Publication Data
Humphrey, James Harry, 1911-
    Helping children manage stress : a guide for adults / James H.
Humphrey.
        p.   cm.
    Includes bibliographical references.
    ISBN 0-87868-668-1
    1. Stress management for children.   2. Stress in children.
3. Child rearing.   I. Title.
BF723.S75H846   1998   98-25980
649'.1--dc21   CIP

Contents

Foreword

Although there has been an overabundance of books and articles devoted to stress over the past two decades, their major focus has been on the effects of stress on adults. The importance of dealing with stress in children has recently attracted increased attention, as it has become apparent that effective interventions at an early age can prevent many disturbances that surface later in life. In addition, the severity of stress in children has escalated dramatically. Many mistakenly believe that such problems are predominantly limited to urban or inner city areas. A survey of more than 4,000 Kansas rural elementary schools students revealed, however, that almost half experienced severe stress behaviors, including "headaches, inability to sleep, fingernail biting, stomachaches, short tempers, and agitation about doing well in school."

A New Orleans poll of elementary school children reported that 90% had witnessed violence, 70% had seen a handgun used, and 40% had actually seen a corpse resulting from a crime. In Los Angeles, as many as 1 out of 5 homicides are witnessed by children, and 10% percent of children treated in the primary pediatric care clinic of a Boston hospital had witnessed a shooting or stabbing before the age of 6, half on the streets and half at home. In New York City, it is not unusual to read about infants and children who have been shot or killed by stray bullets on a weekly basis.

Posttraumatic Stress Disorder is increasingly being seen in children who have been involved in or witnessed vicious crimes, and this disorder may persist through adult life. Fierce competitiveness, hostility, aggression, and other behaviors are often readily apparent at the nursery school level. It is now not unusual to see anxiety attacks in 9-year-olds and stress-induced ulcers at 11. Disruptive family relationships, child abuse, single parent families, and poverty have reached epidemic proportions. More than 1 out of 3 children have no health insurance, 2 out of 5 are born to single mothers, and almost half under the age of 6 live at or below the poverty level.

This sorely needed volume clearly and carefully explains what adults can do to prevent and minimize the harmful consequences of stress. In the first section, the author reviews the general causes of stress, with particular emphasis on problems that originate at home (due to family difficulties) and at school (due to peer, parental, and teacher pressures). The major purpose of this book, however, is to teach adults how they can learn to recognize when they need to intervene to help children manage their emotions and develop effective coping skills.

The second part of the book provides standard stress reduction techniques that adults can use with children. The most popular techniques are adaptations of the "relaxation response," meditation, progressive muscular relaxation, and various types of biofeedback, all of which are covered in detail. The author introduces a novel approach to use at the elementary school level: "story games," which are presented in the form of a story that can be read to a group of children. These games are designed to engage children in a fun activity, and they usually involve contrasting tension-relaxation exercises that reduce tension and muscle spasm. Dr. Humphrey presents various techniques in a comprehensive fashion, and it is easy to understand how their appeal to young children facilitates achieving the desired results. Other chapters cover stress reduction approaches using visual imagery and creative movement to produce general and specific relaxation effects.

Dr. Humphrey's extensive background in educational activities, and particularly his expertise in the field of stress, is evident throughout this work. It could not have come at a more propitious time, and should be required reading for all adults who have caregiving responsibilities for children.

Paul J. Rosch, M.D., F.A.C.P.
President, The American Institute of Stress
Clinical Professor of Medicine and Psychiatry
New York Medical College

Acknowledgments

A book is seldom the sole product of the author. Granted, the author does most of the things concerned with actually putting a book together, from the germ of the idea to seeing it through final publication. It is almost always true, however, that many individuals participate, at least indirectly in some way, before a book is finally "put to bed." This volume is no exception. In this regard, I want to express my sincere appreciation to the hundreds of children and adults who willingly gave their time to participate in my extensive interviews and surveys. This source has been extremely valuable in providing a practical database for the book.

Introduction

Many persons believe stress in children does not begin to be important until a child is able to walk and talk. There is no question, however, that before this stage of development many children will be victims of some sort of stress. In fact, we now know that fetuses respond to maternal stress and that newborns may respond to stress that develops in their parents when the newborn fails to grow or suffers from colic.

In the past, we believed that infants are unaware of the differences between their self and their physical and social environments. Many child development specialists, however, feel that the two most important tasks of the infant and the child up to the age of 2 are to establish inner images of the people and objects in their outer world. In the process of establishing such images, life can be unpleasant for this age cohort, and, as a result, they may become stressed.

Unquestionably, children at all the early age levels, beginning at birth (and possible before), are likely to encounter a considerable amount of stress that our complex modern society generates. The objective of those adults who deal with children should be to help them reduce distress by making a change in the environment and/or making a change in the children themselves.

Not all problems concerned with childhood stress are necessarily evident in the adult population. One such problem is that children are not as likely to be able to cope with stress as successfully as adults, because they do not have the readily available options that adults might have. For example, it seems acceptable for an adult to be angry with a child, but a child is not supposed to display anger with an adult. Also, adults have the option of withdrawing or walking away, but this same freedom may not be available to children.

Another problem is that adults ordinarily fail to recognize the incidence and magnitude of stress in the lives of children. For example, studies have shown that parents perceive children as having lower levels of stress than children perceive themselves as having. There is no question that children face unending challenges and demands in the process of their development.

In order to deal effectively with the problem of childhood stress, adults must apply certain general principles to their own lifestyles. The following such principles are suggested guidelines:

- Maintain healthy practices in nutrition, rest, and exercise.

- Make a continuous effort to take stock of yourself.

- Learn to recognize your own accomplishments.

- Learn to take one thing at a time.

- Learn to take things less seriously.

- Do things for others.

- Talk things over with others.

- Don't confuse stress with challenge.

Part 1:

Understanding Stress in Children

Glossary

ACTH: <u>A</u>dreno<u>c</u>orti<u>c</u>o<u>t</u>ropic <u>h</u>ormone secreted by the pituitary gland. It influences the function of the adrenals and other glands in the body.

Adrenalin: A hormone secreted by the medulla of the adrenal glands.

Adrenals: Two glands in the upper posterior part of the abdomen that produce and secrete hormones. They have two parts, the outer layer, called the **cortex**, and the inner core, called the **medulla**.

Corticoids: Hormones produced by the adrenal cortex, an example of which is **cortisone**.

Endocrine: Glands that secrete their hormones into the blood stream.

Hormone: A chemical produced by a gland, secreted into the blood stream, and influencing the function of cells or organs.

Hypothalamus: The primary activator of the autonomic nervous system, it plays a central role in translating neurological stimuli into endocrine processes during stress reactions.

Pituitary: An endocrine gland about the size of a pea located at the base of the brain. It secretes important hormones, one of which is the ACTH hormone.

Thymus: A ductless gland that is considered a part of the endocrine gland system, located behind the upper part of the breast bone.

Chapter 1
Stress and Child Development

If adults are to be successful in their efforts to help children manage stress, it is important that they have some understanding of the meaning of stress. Although there are various theories of stress, one that is well known and widely accepted is that of Hans Selye (the "Father of Stress") whose model, known as the general adaptation syndrome, consists of three stages: alarm reaction, resistance stage, and the exhaustion stage.

- In the first stage (alarm reaction), the body reacts to the stressor, and that response causes the hypothalamus to produce a biochemical "messenger," which in turn causes the pituitary gland to secrete the hormone ACTH into the blood. The ACTH secretion then stimulates the adrenal gland to discharge adrenalin and other corticoids. These corticoids cause the thymus to shrink, which in turn affects heart rate, blood pressure, and the like. It is during the alarm stage that body resistance is reduced.

- In the second stage, the body develops resistance if the stressor is not too pronounced. The body adapts to the stressful situation, fights back the stress or possibly avoids it, and then begins to repair any damage.

- The third stage, exhaustion, occurs if there is long-term, continuous exposure to the same stressor. The body's ability to adapt is eventually exhausted, and the signs of the first stage (alarm reaction) reappear. Selye contends that our adaptation resources are limited, and, when the depletion becomes irreversible, the result is death [Selye 1975, p. 24].

As in the case of all research, more and more precise and sophisticated procedures will emerge in the scientific study of stress. In the meantime, there is abundant evidence to support the notion that stress in modern society is a most serious threat to human well-being if it is not controlled. [Humphrey 1982].

What these various reactions mean is that the organism is gearing up for a response to a stressor. This phenomenon is called the "fight or flight" response that prepares us for action in the same way that it did for prehistoric man when he was confronted with an enemy. The responses are based on a particular situation, such as fighting an opponent for food or fleeing from an animal that overmatched him. Modern man still experiences these same physiological responses when facing stressful situations. While we generally do not need to fight physically (although we might feel like it sometimes) or to run from wild animals, our bodies still react with the same fight or flight response. Physiologists point out that we need this self-preservation reaction occasionally, but not in response to the emotional traumas and anxieties of modern living.

We can separate physical stress into two general types: emergency stress and continuing stress. In emergency stress, the process described on page 3 takes place. That is, when an emergency arises, such as bodily injury, hormones are discharged into the blood stream, which causes an increase in heart rate, rise in blood pressure, and dilation of the blood vessels in the muscles to prepare themselves for immediate use of the energy that is generated.

In continuing stress, the body reaction is somewhat more complex. The physiological involvement is the same, but more and more hormones continue to be produced to increase body resistance. In some cases where the stress is excessive, such as an extensive third-degree burn, another phase—exhaustion of the adrenal gland—can develop, sometimes culminating in fatality.

Physical Stress

Physical stress can also be the result of unusual and excessive physical exertion. This can be demonstrated by performing an experiment involving some mild physical exertion. First, try to find your resting pulse by placing your right wrist, palm facing you, in your left hand. Now, bring the index and middle fingers of your left hand around the wrist and press lightly until you feel the beat of your pulse.

Next, count the beats for 10 seconds and then multiply this figure by 6. This is your resting pulse rate per minute. For example, if you counted 12 beats in 10 seconds, your resting pulse will be 72 beats per minute. The next step is to engage in some physical activity. Stand and balance yourself on one foot. Hop up and down on this foot for a period of about 20 seconds, or less if that is too strenuous. Then take your pulse again in the same manner.

You will find that, as a result of this activity, your pulse will be higher than your resting pulse. Even with this small amount of physical exertion, the body was adjusting to cope with it, as evidenced by the rise in pulse rate. You were able to discern this yourself; however, other things (such as a slight rise in blood pressure) were likely involved that you were not aware of.

Psychological Stress

The essential difference between physical stress and psychological stress is that the former involves a real situation, while psychological stress is more concerned with foreseeing or imagining an emergency situation. As an example, a vicarious experience of danger may be of sufficient intensity to cause muscle tension and elevate the heart rate. A specific example of psychological stress is seen in what is commonly called "stage fright." Incidentally, it is interesting to note that this type of psychological stress may start when one is a child. For example, my studies of stress-inducing factors among children have indicated that "getting up in front of the class" is an incident that causes much concern and worry to a large number of children.

It has been clearly demonstrated that prolonged and unrelenting nervous tension developing from psychological stress can result in psychosomatic disorders, which in turn can cause serious diseases.

Child Development

For us to help children manage stress, we must not only understand stress itself, but also principles of child development. All children are going to experience some sort of stress, although many may never have to contend with more than the average amount of stress that is caused by growth and development. Other children, however, may be encumbered with such serious life stressors as divorce, hospitalization, or a death in the family.

Some children seem to encounter few problems in coping with stress. They recover quickly and are able to incorporate the stressful experience into their everyday experiences. They have a great deal of confidence in themselves and when they encounter a stressful situation and cope with it successfully, their self-confidence increases.

Some children can cope with stress to some extent, but they have to work at it. They gain more self-confidence as they improve their ability to cope. They do seem to have as high a level of success, however, as those classified as "exceptional copers."

Other children have a great deal of difficulty coping with stress. They have problems struggling with some of the processes of normal growth and development. In addition, they become upset and disorganized by the daily hassles as well as stressful events.

The aim of adults, of course, should be to help children become successful in managing stress. With some knowledge of child development, adults should be better able to provide environments that will help children effectively manage stress during their developmental years.

Total Child Development

Total development is sum of all the physical, social, emotional, and intellectual components of any individual, and all of these components are highly interrelated and interdependent. All are important for well-being. When a nervous child stutters or becomes nauseated, a mental state is not necessarily causing a physical symptom. The total organism is upset by a particular situation and reflects its upset in several ways, including disturbance in thought, feeling, and body processes. The whole child interacts with the social and physical environment, and as the child is affected by the environment, he or she in turn has an effect upon it.

Physical Development

A child's body is something he can see. It is his base of operation. The other components of total development—social, emotional, and intellectual—are somewhat vague to him. Consequently, it is important to help a child to gain some degree of control over his body early in life (what is known as basic body control). The ability to do this, of course, will vary from one child to another and will likely depend upon the child's physical fitness, which consists of muscular strength, endurance and power, circulatory-respiratory endurance, agility, speed, flexibility, balance, and coordination.

Social Development

Human beings are social beings. They work together for the benefit of society. They have fought together in times of crisis, and they play together. Social development, however, is quite vague and confusing, particularly where children are concerned.

While it is a relatively easy matter to identify certain components of physical fitness, such as strength and endurance, the same is not true for components of social fitness. The components of physical fitness are the same for children as for adults. The components of social fitness for children, however, may be different from the components of adult social fitness. By some adult standards, children might be considered as social misfits, because certain child behaviors are not socially acceptable to some adults.

Emotional Development

An emotion is the response an individual makes when confronted with a situation for which he or she is unprepared, or which is interpreted as a possible source of gain or loss. There are pleasant emotions, such as joy, and those that are unpleasant, like fear. (It is interesting to note that a good proportion of the literature is devoted to emotions that are unpleasant. Psychology texts give much more space to such emotional patterns as fear, hate, and guilt, than to such pleasant emotions as love, sympathy, and contentment.)

Generally speaking, the pleasantness or unpleasantness of an emotion seems to be determined by its strength or intensity, by the nature of the situation arousing it, and by the way a child perceives or interprets the situation. The emotions of young children tend to be more intense than those of adults. If adults are not aware of this aspect of child behavior, they will not be likely to understand why a child reacts rather violently to a situation that to them seems somewhat insignificant. Adults should also take into account the fact that different children will react differently to the same type of situation. For example, something that might anger one child might have a rather passive influence on another.

Intellectual Development

Children possess varying degrees of intelligence, and most fall within a range of what is called "normal" intelligence. Because of the somewhat vague nature of intelligence, it is practically impossible to identify specific components of it. Thus, we need to view intellectual fitness in a somewhat different manner than physical or social fitness.

I consider intellectual fitness by looking at how certain things influence intelligence. If we know this, then we might understand better how to contribute to intellectual fitness by improving upon some of these factors. Some of the factors that tend to influence intelligence are health and physical condition, emotional disturbance, certain social and economic factors, and stress. When adults recognize these factors, perhaps they will be able to deal more satisfactorily with children in helping them in their intellectual pursuits.

Stages of Child Development

The descriptions of the various stages of child development reflect the characteristics of the so-called "average" child. Although children are more alike than they are different, they all differ in at least one or more characteristics, even identical twins. Therefore, the reader is reminded that the general traits and characteristics included in the following discussion are suggestive of the behavior of the "average" child. If a given child does not conform to these characteristics, it does not mean that he or she is seriously deviating from the norm. Each child progresses at his or her own rate and there is likely to be overlapping from one stage of development to another.

Birth to 15 Months

The first stage of development is the period from birth to 15 months. This can be determined as the "intake" stage, because behavior and growth is characterized by taking in not only food, but also such other things as sound, light, and the various forms of total care.

Separation anxiety can occur at this stage. Since the child is entirely dependent upon the mother or other caregiver for meeting needs, the child sees separation as being deprived of these important needs. It is at this stage that the child's caregiver (ordinarily the parent) should try to maintain a proper balance between meeting the child's needs and overgratification. Many child development specialists seem to agree that children who experience stress from separation, or from having to wait for a need to be fulfilled, are gaining the opportunity to organize their psychological resources and adapt to stress. On the contrary, children who do not have this balance may be those who tend to disorganize under stress. They fall into the previously mentioned third level of classification of children who have a great deal of difficulty coping with stress.

15 Months to 3 Years

Children develop autonomy between the ages of 15 months to 3 years. This can be described as the "I am what I do" stage. Autonomy develops because most children can now move about rather easily. The child does not have to rely entirely on a caregiver to meet every single need. Autonomy also results from the development of mental processes, because the child can think about things and put language to use.

It is during this stage that toilet training can be a major stressor. Children are not always given the needed opportunity to express autonomy during this process. It can be a difficult time for the child, because he is ordinarily expected to cooperate with and gain the approval of the principal caregiver. If the child cooperates and uses the toilet, approval is forthcoming; however, some autonomy is lost. If he does not cooperate, disapproval may result. If this conflict is not resolved satisfactorily, some clinical psychologists believe it will emerge during adulthood in the form of highly anxious and compulsive behaviors.

3 to 5 Years

The next period, from 3 to 5 years, can be described as the "I am what I think I am" stage. Children use body movement skills in a more purposeful way. Children develop the ability to daydream and make believe, and pretending allows them to be what they want to be—anything from animals to astronauts. It is possible, however, that resorting to fantasy may result in stress, because children may become scared of their own fantasies.

5 to 7 Years

The age level from 5 through 7 years usually includes children from kindergarten through second grade. During this period, the child begins his formal education. In our culture, he leaves the home for a part of the day to take his place in a classroom with children of approximately the same age. Not only is he taking an important step toward becoming more independent and self-reliant, but he moves from being a highly self-centered individual to becoming a more socialized member of the group. Some children are stressed by separation anxiety when they make the transition from home to school.

This stage is usually characterized by a certain lack of motor coordination, because the small muscles of the hands and fingers are not as well developed as the large muscles of the arms and legs. Thus, as he starts his formal education, the child needs to use large crayons or pencils as one way to express himself. His urge to action is expressed through movement, since he lives in a moving world, so to speak. Children at these age levels thrive on vigorous activity. They develop as they climb, run, jump, hop, skip, or keep time to music. An important physical aspect at this state is that the eyeball is increasing in size and the eye muscles are developing. This factor is an important determinant in the child's readiness to see and read small print, and, thus, it involves a progression from large print on charts to smaller type in primers.

Even though he has a relatively short attention span, the child is extremely curious about the environment. At this stage, adults can capitalize upon the child's urge to learn by providing opportunities for him to gain information from firsthand experiences. He sees, hears, smells, feels, and even tastes in order to learn.

8 to 9 Years

The age range from 8 to 9 years is the stage that usually marks the time spent in the third and fourth grade. The child now has a wider range of interests and a longer attention span. While strongly individualistic, the child is working more from a position in the group. Organized games should afford opportunities for developing and practicing skills in good leadership and followership as well as body control, strength, and endurance. Small muscles are developing, manipulative skills are increasing, and muscular coordination is improving. The eyes have developed to a point where the child can read more widely. The child is capable of getting information from books and is beginning to learn more through vicarious experience. Experiments carry an impact for learning at this stage by capitalizing upon the child's curiosity. This is the stage of the child's development when communication skills (listening, speaking, reading, and writing) and the ability to use numbers are needed to deal with situations both in and out of school.

10 to 12 Years

During the ages of 10 through 12, most children complete fifth and sixth grades. This is a period of transition for most, as they go from childhood into the preadolescent period. They may show concern over body changes and are sometimes self-conscious about appearance. This causes stress for some children. At this stage, children tend to differ widely in physical maturation and emotional stability. Greater deviations in development can be noted within sex groups than between them. Rate of physical growth can be rapid, sometimes showing itself in poor posture and restlessness.

Some of the more highly organized team games such as softball or modified soccer help furnish the keen and wholesome competition desired by children at this stage of development. It is essential that adults recognize that prestige among peers is now more important than adult approval. During this stage, the child should be ready for a higher level of intellectual skills that involve reasoning, discerning fact from opinion, noting cause-and-effect relationships, drawing conclusions, and using various references to locate and compare the validity of information. The child is beginning to show more proficiency in expressing himself through oral and written communication.

Thus, after the child enters school and completes the elementary school years, he or she develops socially, from a self-centered individual to a participating member of a group; emotionally, to a higher degree of self-control; physically, from childhood to the brink of adolescence; and intellectually, from learning through firsthand experiences to learning from more technical and specialized resources. All of these experiences can cause various degrees of stress for some children.

Notes

Humphrey, J. H. (1982). *A textbook of stress*. Springfield, IL: Charles C Thomas.

Selye, H. (1975). *Stress without distress*. New York: Signet New American Library.

Chapter 2
General Causes of Childhood Stress

Almost anything that occurs in life can cause stress to a certain degree. General causes of stress include all of the various factors concerned with our modern, highly technological society, such as the mass media—especially the daily news that bombards us with information that, if taken too seriously, can provide stressful conditions. In addition, overcrowding, air and noise pollution, along with the everyday "hustle and bustle to survive," combine to make life in general a somewhat frustrating experience. All of us, children and adults alike, are possible stress victims of these conditions. Moreover, some of us by the very nature of our specific environments are susceptible to many stress-inducing factors.

When caregivers are aware of some of the causes of stress in children, they should be in a better position to help them manage stress. It is possible for adults to eliminate many of these stress-inducting factors. For those factors that cannot be eliminated entirely, adults should make serious attempts at least to keep them under control. This chapter will identify some of the general causes of stress in children.

During the last several years, various researchers have studied certain life events as causes of stress. They have attempted to find out what kinds of health problems are associated with various events that occur to people either in the normal course of events, or as a result of some sort of misfortune.

Perhaps the first investigator to gather life events data on children was R. Dean Coddington, who was one of my collaborators on an extensive childhood stress project. Following is Coddington's list of life events that cause the most stress for children [Coddington 1984].

1. The death of a parent
2. The death of a brother or sister
3. Divorce of parents
4. Marital separation of parents
5. The death of a grandparent
6. Hospitalization of a parent
7. Remarriage of a parent
8. Birth of brother of sister
9. Hospitalization of a brother or sister
10. Loss of a job by your father or mother
11. Major increase in a parent's income
12. Major decrease in a parent's income
13. Start of a new problem between parents
14. End of a problem between parents
15. Change in a father's job so he has less time at home
16. A new adult moving into the house
17. Mother beginning to work outside the house
18. Being told you are attractive by a friend
19. Beginning the first grade
20. Moving to a new school district
21. Failing a grade in school
22. Suspension from school
23. Start of a new problem between you and your parents
24. End of a problem between you and your parents
25. Recognition for excelling in a sport or other activity
26. Appearing before a juvenile court
27. Failing to achieve something you really want
28. Becoming an adult member of a church
29. Being invited to join a social organization
30. Death of a pet
31. Being hospitalized for illness or injury
32. Death of a close friend
33. Getting involved with drugs
34. Stopping the use of drugs
35. Finding an adult who really respects you
36. Outstanding personal achievement (special prize)

As important as life event scales are as a means of determining causes of stress, they are not without their critics. Some specialists feel that a better measure would be related to day-to-day problems, or "daily hassles." In my own studies of childhood stress, I have collected data on daily stressors of children in four different age ranges. Listed below are the five most common daily hassles of children at these ages.

Ages 5-6

Fighting with my brother
Not knowing what I should do
Starting school
When I have to go to bed early
Having to eat stuff I don't like

Ages 7-8

When my parents don't trust me
When my mother blames me for something I didn't do
Afraid I will fail
Kids who don't like me
Having to do homework

Ages 9-10

When I can't watch TV
When teachers don't treat me like a person
When I don't get credit for something I did
Unfair punishment
Parents who think they know everything

Ages 11-12

Teachers who think they know it all
Not being as strong as I would like to be
Girls who think they are smart
Kids who make fun of me
Wearing my older brother's clothes

Obviously, most of these daily hassles can be dealt with in a suitable manner by alert adults.

Children also have numerous concerns about their place and function in modern society, which may induce stress. The following descriptive list of such factors will alert the reader to these concerns, and facilitate an understanding of some of the things that need to be done in order to assist children to manage stress.

- **Concerns about meeting personal goals**. Stress can result if adults set goals too difficult for children to accomplish. For example, goals may be much higher than a particular home or school environment will permit children to achieve. On the other hand, when goals are set too low, children may develop the feeling that they are not doing as much for themselves as they should. This aspect of stress is also concerned with the fear children have that they will not reach their goals in life. With some children, this can happen early in life.

- **Concerns about self-esteem**. Self-esteem can often be highly related to the fulfillment of certain ego needs. Some children may feel that there are not enough opportunities offered in modern society for them to succeed. This is perhaps more true of children who are in a low socioeconomic environment.

- **Concerns about changing values.** Some children become frustrated when they do not understand the value system imposed on them by some adults. They may develop the feeling that adults are not inclined to place a value on those factors that children believe are personally important to them at their various stages of growth and development.

- **Concerns about social standards.** Some children get confused with the difference in social standards required at the different levels of development. It is sometimes difficult for them to understand that what was socially acceptable at one age level is not necessarily so at another.

- **Concerns about personal competence and ability.** This might well be the concern that frustrates children the most. Certainly, a child's lack of confidence in his ability can be devastating to his morale. Many children are becoming increasingly concerned with their ability, or lack thereof, to cope with such problems as expectations of parents and keeping up with schoolwork.

- **Concerns about personal traits and characteristics.** Not the least of concerns among children are those factors that are likely to make them different from the so-called average or normal child. This has to do with the social need for mutuality, when children want to be like their peers. When children deviate radically from others in certain traits and characteristics, it can be a serious stress-inducing factor.

It should be mentioned that not all of these concerns are characteristic of all children, particularly because of the individual differences among them. What may be a serious concern for one child may be a minimal concern for another. Nonetheless, these concerns can serve as guidelines for adults in some of their dealing with children and in helping them to manage stress.

Notes

Coddington, L. D. (1984). Measuring the stressfulness of a child's environment. In J. H. Humphrey (Ed.), *Stress in childhood.* New York: AMS Press, Inc.

Chapter 3
Stressful Environments

Children in the age range from 5 to 12 spend about two-thirds of their waking hours in the home and the remaining one-third in the school [Humphrey & Humphrey 1989]. This chapter examines certain stressful aspects of these two environments.

Home and Family Stress

The magnitude of home and family stress on children is well-documented [Humphrey 1990]. For example, in the list of stressful life events presented in the previous chapter (see page 16), more than half are concerned with home and family. Without question, changes in society with consequent changes in home conditions are likely to make child adjustment a difficult problem.

Some psychiatrists are convinced that some home conditions can have an extremely negative influence on the personality and mental health of some children, not only at their present stage of growth and development, but in the future as well. In fact, studies show that the interaction of stress factors is especially important. Most of these studies tend to identify the following factors to be strongly associated with child (and possibly later) psychiatric disorders:

- Severe marital discord,

- Low socioeconomic status,

- Overcrowding or large family size,

- Paternal criminality,

- Maternal psychiatric disorder, and

- Admission into the care of local authorities.

It is estimated that, with only one of the above conditions present, a child is no more likely to develop psychiatric problems than any other child. When two of the conditions occur, however, the child's psychiatric risk increases fourfold [Humphrey 1986].

Research also suggests that most children can cope and adapt to the short-term crisis, such as divorce, within a few years. If the stress is compounded by other stresses and continued adversity, however, developmental disorders may occur. Responses to stress are modified by such variables as temperament and personality, developmental status, sex, and support systems.

In Coddington's list, remarriage of a parent is rated high among stressful life events. In fact, the presence of a stepparent may signify a number of other stressors that the child has to contend with; for example, the loss of a father, adjustment to a new parental figure in the home, and conflicting loyalties between "new" fathers and "old" fathers. Several studies suggest that the school-age child is particularly vulnerable to a parent's remarriage, because he or she is old enough to understand that relationships between parent and child have a permanence beyond time and place. In contrast, preschool children often accept the new stepparent as one of the family, since their view of families is more concretely tied to the physical presence of who lives together.

There are certain specific conditions that tend to focus on a single aspect of home and family stress. These are child abuse, divorce and/or separation, and the birth of a siblings. (It should be understood that there is likely to be some overlapping from one of these categories to another.)

Child Abuse

It is estimated that more than 1 million children are abused or neglected by their parents or other caregivers in our country annually, and that 2,000 or more die as a result of maltreatment [Humphrey 1988]. Authorities suggest that most of this is not caused by inhuman, hateful intent on the part of parents, but rather is the result of a combination of factors, including both the accumulation of stresses on families and unmet support needs of parents in coping with their childbearing responsibilities.

Social stressors associated with child abuse include unemployment, lack of social support, stressful life events, and high levels of confusion. Sociological and maternal characteristics are inextricably intertwined in mutual causal relationships in child abuse. Early separation during the postpartum period (failure of bond formation) has been associated with abuse and neglect of mothers.

Although there is a growing body of literature linking stress to child abuse and neglect [Humphrey 1988], the relationship is not unambiguously supported by empirical data. Predisposing factors (which can be grouped into individual, familial, social, and cultural factors) may either positively or negatively affect the potential for child abuse and neglect, depending on the quality of social networks and social support available to families. These factors operate most importantly not between the perception of stress and the act of abuse or neglect, but through the interpretation of whether a given life event is stressful or not. This clarification points the way to redefining interventions for the primary prevention of child abuse and neglect. Existing support systems can be strengthened in order to increase a family's ability to cope with untoward events before these become stressful. In addition, advocacy activities that support children and families in general can be major components in the primary prevention of child abuse and neglect.

Divorce and/or Separation

During the past 25 years, the number of children who have experienced parental divorce has tripled. Although the rate of divorce is expected to increase more slowly in the present decade than the previous one, it is estimated that by the year 2000, one-third or more of all children will have experienced parental divorce during childhood or adolescence [Wolchik 1984].

Depression, anger, self-blame, anxiety, and low self-esteem frequently occur after divorce. In addition, social interaction problems, noncompliance, aggression, and school difficulties occur more frequently among children of divorce than children from intact families. For some children, divorce produces mild or transient behavior problems, but for many others, this transition in family structure leads to enduring emotional and behavioral difficulties.

Much of the confusion in studying the impact of divorce on children may be the result of failure to view divorce as a process involving a series of events and changes in life circumstances, rather than as a single event. At different points in this sequence, children are confronted with different adaptive tasks and will use different coping strategies. The diversity of children's responses to divorce in part is attributable to temperamental status. In understanding the child's adjustment to divorce, it is important to look not only at changes in family structure, but also at changes in family functioning and at stresses and support systems in the child's extrafamilial social environment.

Siblings

The fear that some children have of the prospect of being replaced by, or at the least, taking a back seat to, a new arrival can be stress inducing. Since the average American family has at least two children, this is a problem that most families will need to deal with. The extent to which sibling rivalry can be stress inducing varies a great deal from one family to another. It is certainly a condition that a parent should be able to control if he or she wishes to do so.

My own studies of traits and characteristics of children show that sibling feelings can change from one age level to another. For example, on the average, the 5-year-old seldom shows jealousy toward younger siblings. A year later, however, he may show jealousy at times, but at other times he may take pride in siblings.

School Stress

In Coddington's list of stressful events, more than 10% are concerned with the school environment, and they are heavily weighted as being stressful to children. Indeed, there are a number of conditions existing in many school situations that can cause much stress in children. These conditions prevail at all levels—possibly in different ways—from the time a child enters school until graduation from college. School anxiety as a child stressor is a phenomenon with which educators, particularly teachers and counselors, frequently find themselves confronted with in dealing with children. Various theories have been advanced to explain this phenomenon and relate it to other character traits and emotional dispositions. Literature on the subject reveals the following characteristics of anxiety as a stress-inducing factor in the education process [Humphrey & Humphrey 1986]:

- Anxiety is considered a learnable reaction that has the properties of a response, a cue of danger, and a drive.

- Anxiety is internalized fear aroused by the memory of painful past experiences associated with punishment.

- Anxiety in the classroom interferes with learning, and whatever can be done to reduce it should serve as a spur to learning.

- Test anxiety is a near universal experience, especially in this country, which is a test-giving and test-conscious culture.

- Evidence from clinical studies points clearly and consistently to the disruptive and distracting power of anxiety effects over most kinds of thinking [Humphrey 1990].

Causes of anxiety change with age, as do perceptions of stressful situations. Adults should take care in assessing the total life space of the child—background, home life, school life, age, and sex—in order to minimize the anxiety experienced in the school. It seems obvious that school anxiety, although manifested in the school environment, may often be caused by unrelated factors outside the school.

Starting to School

One of the most stressful life events for some young children is beginning the first grade. One of the reasons for this may possibly be that older childhood friends, siblings, and even some unthinking parents admonish the child with, "Wait until you get to school; you're going to get it." This kind of negative attitude is likely to increase any separation anxiety that the child already has.

Chapter 1 indicated that such separation anxiety begins in the first stage of a child's development, from birth to 15 months. It can reach a peak at the latter part of the development stage from 3 to 5 years, because it is the child's first attempt to become a part of the outer world: the school. For many children, this is the first task of enforced separation. For those who do not have a well-developed sense of continuity, the separation might be easily equated with the loss of the life-sustaining mother. The stress associated with such a disaster could be overwhelming for such a child. Learning to tolerate the stress of separation is one of the central concerns of preschoolers; adults should be alert to signs, seek to lessen the impact, and work out compromises, not necessarily to remove the stress, but to help the child gradually build a tolerance for separation.

In extreme cases of the separation problem, a child's reaction typically may include temper tantrums, crying, screaming, and refusal to go to school. Or, in some instances, suspiciously sudden aches and pains might serve to keep the "sick" child home. What the child is reacting against is not the school, but separation from the mother. The child may see the stress associated with this event as a devastating loss equated with being abandoned. The child's behavior in dealing with the stress can be so extreme as to demand special treatment on the part of the significant adults in his life.

The aim in such cases should always be to ease the transition into school. Keep in mind that separation is a two-way street. Assuring parents of the competency of the school staff and of the physical safety of their child may go a long way toward helping to lessen the stress. If adults act responsibly and with consistency, the child should be able to make an adequate adjustment to this daily separation from family and, in the process, learn an important lesson in meeting reality demands.

School Competition

In a study I conducted with 200 fifth- and sixth-grade children, one of the questions I asked was, "What is the one thing that worries you most in school?" As might be expected, there was a variety of responses. The one general characteristic that tended to emerge, however, was the emphasis on competition in so many school situations.

Most of the literature on competition for children has focused on sports activities [Humphrey 1993]; however, there are many situations that exist in some classrooms that can cause classroom stress. An example is the antiquated "Spelling Bee," which still exists in some schools, and in fact, continues to be recognized in an annual national competition. Perhaps the first few children "spelled down" are likely to be the ones who need spelling practice the most. And, to say the least, it can be embarrassing to fail in any school task in front of others.

The reconciliation of children's competitive needs and cooperative needs is not an easy matter. In a sense, we are confronted with an ambivalent condition that, if not handled carefully, could place children in a state of conflict, thus causing them to suffer distress. Society not only rewards one kind of behavior (cooperation), but also its direct opposite (competition). Perhaps more often than not, our cultural demands sanction these rewards without provision of clear-cut standards of value with regard to specific conditions under which these forms of behavior might well be practiced. Thus, the child is placed in something of a quandary as to when to compete and when to cooperate.

Based on my own experience and examination of the available evidence, the following concepts seem justifiable:

- Very young children in general are not competitive, but become more so as they grow older.

- There is a wide variety in competition among children; some are violently competitive, while others are mildly competitive, and still others are not competitive at all.

- Boys tend to be more competitive than girls.

- Competition should be adjusted so that there is not a preponderant number of winners over losers.

- Competition and rivalry produce results in effort and speed of accomplishment.

Those who deal with children at the various age levels might well be guided by the above concepts. It might be kept in mind that competition should not necessarily be restrained. On the other hand, it should be kept under control, so that competitive needs of children are met in a satisfactory and wholesome manner.

Academic Subjects

There are various subject areas considered to be perennial nemeses for many students. In fact, if you ask an elementary school child what he likes best in school, the traditional response has invariably been recess and lunch. Of course, neither of these are bona fide subjects, and many children, when pressed, will respond with what they hate the least.

Probably any subject could be stress inducing for certain students. For many children, attending school daily and performing poorly is a source of considerable and prolonged stress. If the children overreact to environmental stresses in terms of increased muscle tension, this may easily interfere with the fluid muscular movement required in handwriting tasks, decreasing their performance and further increasing environmental stresses. Most educators have seen children squeeze their pencils tightly, press hard on their paper, purse their lips, and tighten their bodies, using an inordinate amount of energy and concentration to write while performing at a low level.

Reading is one area of school activity that is loaded with anxiety, stress, and frustration for many children. In fact, reading specialists recognize the "frustration level" in teaching children to read. In terms of behavioral observation, this is the level at which children evidence distracting tension, excessive or erratic body movements, nervousness, and distractibility. This frustration level is said to be a sign of emotional tension or stress that results in breakdowns in fluency and a significant increase in reading errors.

Mathematics tends to be another stressful subject. This condition prevails from the study of arithmetic upon entering school through the required courses in mathematics in college. This has become such a problem in recent years that there is now an area of study called "Math Anxiety" that is receiving increasing attention [Humphrey & Humphrey 1990a].

Teachers who make an effort to reduce the number of stressful situations in mathematics programs will not only be helping their students to become better mathematics learners, but at the same time they will also be helping them to be more confident and capable performers in mathematical tasks as adults.

School Tests

In more than 40 years as a teacher, which included all levels from elementary school through the university graduate school, I have observed many students who were seriously stressed by "test phobia," or what has now become known as test anxiety.

Perceived stress appears to depend on psychological responses that individuals are more likely to bring to the testing situation than to manufacture on the spot. Students respond to tests and testing situations with learned patterns of stress reactivity. The patterns may vary among individuals and may reflect differences in autonomic nervous system conditioning; feelings of threat or worry regarding the symbolic meaning of the test or the testing situation; and/or coping skills that govern the management of complexity, frustration, information load, symbolic manipulation, and mobilization of resources. There are also individual patterns of maladaptive behavior such as anxiety, a sustained high level of autonomic activity after exposure to a stressor, and the use of such defense mechanisms as learned helplessness and avoidance behavior.

Perceived stress also depends upon the nature of the task to be performed. As tasks get more complex and require greater degrees of coordination and integration of the nervous system, a given stressor level will affect task performance as if it were a stronger stressor.

On the basis of my own experience and an extensive review of the literature on test anxiety, the following generalizations seem warranted:

- If the test is considered important to the individual, and if he is anxious when taking tests, he is more likely to perform poorly on tests than a person who is less anxious.

- Students from a low socioeconomic level tend to be most anxious when facing a test.

- Those who are least anxious when facing a test tend to be those who have the least need or desire to do well on it.

- Although extreme anxiety is likely to interfere with test performance, mild anxiety can facilitate test performance.

- The more familiar a student is with tests of a particular type, the less likely he is to suffer extreme anxiety.

- Test anxiety can enhance learning if it is distributed at a relatively low level throughout a course of instruction, rather than being concentrated at a relatively high level just prior to and during the test.

- There are low-to-moderate negative relationships between measures of anxiety and performance on complex tasks. This negative relationship tends to increase with grade level and appears to be long range, rather than transitory.

It is important to take a positive attitude when considering test results. That is, emphasis should be placed on the number of answers that are correct. For example, the child will more likely be encouraged if you say, "You got seven right," rather than, "You missed three." There is evidence to show that this approach can help to minimize stress in test taking.

Schools and Gender Differences

In general, emotional stress seems to have a greater effect on boys than on girls in both the school and home environment. One possible exception to this at school is that girls are prone to suffer more anxiety over report cards than are boys [Humphrey & Humphrey 1990b]. Most studies show that boys are much more likely to be stressed by family discord and disruption than are girls, although there does not seem to be a completely satisfactory explanation for this. In fact, many people have been critical of the early school learning environment, particularly as far as boys are concerned. Some of these critics have gone so far as to say that young boys are being discriminated against in their early school years.

A generally accepted description of the term *learning* is that it involves some sort of change in behavior. Many learning theorists maintain that behavior is a product of heredity and environment. The issue here is whether or not an environment is provided that is best suited for learning for young boys at the early age levels, and further, whether such an environment is likely to cause more stress among young boys than girls.

While the school has no control over ancestry, it can, within certain limitations, exercise some degree of control over the kind of environment in which the learner must function. Generally speaking, it is doubtful that all schools have provided an environment that is most conducive to learning as far as young boys are concerned. Many child development specialists have characterized the environment at the primary level of education as feminized.

A major factor to consider concerns the biological differences between boys and girls in this particular age range, and it is questionable whether educational planning has always taken these important differences into account. Over the years, there has been an accumulation of evidence on this general subject appearing in the literature on child development, some of which is summarized here, along with some of my own personal observations [Humphrey & Humphrey 1990b].

Due to certain male hormonal conditions, boys tend to be more aggressive, restless, and impatient. In addition, the male has more rugged bone structure, and as a consequence has greater strength than the female at all ages. Because of this, males tend to display greater muscular reactivity that in turn expresses itself in a stronger tendency toward restlessness and vigorous overt activity.

Another factor is the difference in basal metabolic rate (BMR) in young boys and girls. The BMR is indicative of the speed at which body fuel is changed into energy, as well as how fast this energy is used. The BMR can be measured in terms of calories per meter of body surface with a calorie representing a unit measure of heat energy in food. On average, BMR rises from birth to about 3 years of age and then starts to decline until the ages of 20 to 24. The BMR is higher for boys than for girls, particularly at the early age levels. Because of the higher BMR, boys in turn will have a higher amount of energy to expend, so it appears logical to assume that these factors will influence the male in his behavior patterns.

From a growth and development point of view, the female is actually a much better developed organism, although at birth she is from one-half to one centimeter less in length than the male and around 300 grams less in weight. When she enters school, the female is usually 6 to 12 months more physically mature than the male. As a result, girls may be likely to learn earlier how to perform tasks of manual dexterity, such as buttoning their clothing. In one of my own observational studies of school children, I found that little girls were able to perform the task of tying their shoelaces at a rate of almost four times that of little boys.

Although all schools should not be categorized in the same manner, many of them are tradition bound and ordinarily provide an environment that places emphasis upon neatness, orderliness, and passivity, which are easier for girls to conform to than boys. Of course, this may be partly because our culture has tended to force females to be identified with many of these characteristics.

The authoritarian and sedentary classroom atmosphere is frequently the "sit still and listen" situation, which fails to take into account the greater activity drive and physical aggressiveness of boys. What have been characterized as feminization traits, prevailing in some elementary schools, tend to have an adverse influence on the young male child's learning.

Some studies have shown that, with respect to hyperactivity, boys may outnumber girls by a ratio of as much as 9 to 1 [Humphrey 1988]. This may be one of the reasons why teachers generally tend to rate young males as being so much more aggressive than females, with the result that young boys are considered to be more negative and extroverted. Because of these characteristics, boys generally have poorer relationships with their teachers than girls and, in the area of behavior problems and discipline in the age range from 5 to 8 years, boys account for twice as many disturbances as girls. The importance of this factor is borne out when it is considered that good teacher-pupil relationships tend to raise the achievement levels of both sexes.

Various studies have shown that girls generally receive higher grades than boys, although boys may achieve as well as, and in some cases better, than girls [Humphrey 1988]. It is also clearly evident that boys in the early years fail twice as often as girls, even when there is no significant difference between intelligence and achievement test scores of both sexes. This suggests that even though both sexes have the same intellectual tools, there are other factors that work against learning as far as boys are concerned.

If we are willing to accept the research findings and observational evidence appearing in the child development literature, then the question is: "What attempts, if any, are being made to improve the condition?" At one time it was thought that the solution might lie in a defeminization of the schools at the early age levels by putting more men into classrooms as teachers. But this seems to have met with little success, because the learning environment remains essentially the same regardless of the sex of the teacher. Some educators have suggested that boys start school later, or that girls start earlier. The problem with this, of course, is that state laws concerned with school entrance are likely to distinguish only in terms of age, not sex. In a few remote instances, some schools have experimented with separating boys and girls at the early grade levels. In some cases, this form of grouping has resulted in both groups achieving at a higher level than when the sexes were in class together.

Another major question is, "What can be done at least partially to restructure an environment that will be more favorable to young boys' learning?" One step in this direction recommended by various child development specialists is to develop curriculum content that is more action oriented, thus taking into account the basic need for motor activity [Humphrey 1992]. School personnel might consider learning activities that encourage boys to use excess energy. We do not know whether this kind of curriculum content would make learning less stressful for boys. My own experimentation with the use of body movements to develop academic skills and concepts, however, has shown definite possibilities along these lines.

Stress can be induced in children whose teachers are themselves under stress. This has been a problem for many years and, more than three decades ago, researchers estimated that, based on minimum incidence statistics and pupil-teacher ratios, anxiety may affect as many as 200,000 teachers, and through them 5 million students [Humphrey & Humphrey 1986]. The situation does not appear to be improving, what with relatively large numbers of children, even of elementary school age, bringing guns and other weapons to school.

The second section of this book presents specific strategies for reducing stress in children. These strategies involve relaxation, stunt games, creative movement, and imagery.

Notes

Humphrey, J. H. (1986). *Profiles in stress*. New York: AMS Press, Inc.

Humphrey, J. H. (1988). *Children and stress*. New York: AMS Press, Inc.

Humphrey, J. H. (1990). Research in childhood stress in the home and family and school environment. In J. H. Humphrey (Ed.), *Human stress: Current selected research* (Vol. 3). New York: AMS Press, Inc.

Humphrey, J. H. (1992). *Motor learning in childhood education*. Springfield, IL: Charles C Thomas Publisher.

Humphrey, J. H. (1993). *Sports for children*. Springfield, IL: Charles C Thomas Publisher.

Humphrey, J. H., & Humphrey, J. N. (1990a). *Mathematics can be child's play*. Springfield, IL: Charles C Thomas Publisher.

Humphrey, J. H., & Humphrey, J. N. (1990b). *Reading can be child's play*. Springfield, IL: Charles C Thomas Publisher.

Humphrey, J. N., & Humphrey, J. H. (1986). *Coping with stress in teaching*. New York: AMS Press, Inc.

Humphrey, J. N., & Humphrey, J. H. (1989). *Child development during the elementary school years*. Springfield, IL: Charles C Thomas Publisher.

Wolchik, S. A. et al. (1984). Environmental change and children of divorce. In J. H. Humphrey (Ed.), *Stress in childhood*. New York: AMS Press, Inc.

Part 2
Managing Stress in Children

Chapter 4
Physical Activity and Exercise

Until relatively recent years, we have been aware only of the vast importance of physical activity and exercise to cardiovascular and muscular endurance, which improved physical fitness. We now know that regular exercise has important psychological benefits as well, because it can decrease anxiety and increase self-confidence and self-esteem. This is accomplished because exercise helps the body manufacture and release natural drugs that provide what is known as a "high." This occurs because exercise causes morphine-like chemicals (endogenous opioids) to be released by the hormonal system.

Generally speaking, there are three types of activities that are useful in improving physical fitness: proprioceptive-facilitative, isotonic, and isometric.

Proprioceptive-Facilitative Activities

These activities consist of the various refined patterns of movement that are found in various active games. Important in the performance of these activities are those factors involved in movement: time, force, space, and flow.

Time is concerned with how long it takes to complete a movement. For example, a movement can be slow and deliberate, such as a child attempting to create his or her own body movement to depict a falling snowflake. On the other hand, a movement might be made with sudden quickness, such as starting to run for a goal on a signal.

Force needs to be applied to set the body or one of its segments in motion, as well as to change its speed and/or direction. Thus, force is concerned with how much strength is required for movement. Swinging an arm requires less strength than attempting to propel the body over the surface area with a standing long jump.

In general, there are two factors concerned with *space*. These are the amount of space required to perform a particular movement and the use of available space.

All movements involve some degree of rhythm in their performance. Thus, *flow* is the sequence of movement involving rhythmic motion.

The above factors are included in most all body movements in various degrees. The degree to which each is used effectively in combination will determine the extent to which the movement is performed with skill. This is a basic essential in the performance of proprioceptive-facilitative activities. In addition, various combinations of the following features are involved in the performance of this type of activity: muscular power, agility, speed, flexibility, balance, and coordination.

Isotonic Activities

Isotonic activities are the type of activities that most people are familiar with. An isotonic activity involves the amount of resistance you can overcome during one application of force through the full range of motion in a given joint or joints. An example of this would be picking up a weight and flexing the elbows while lifting the weight to shoulder height.

Isotonics can improve strength to some extent. They are also useful for increasing and maintaining a full range of motion. Such range of motion should be maintained throughout life if possible, although it can decrease with age and with some musculoskeletal disorders such as arthritis.

Another important feature of isotonic activity is that it can increase circulatory-respiratory endurance in such activities as running and swimming. These activities are usually referred to as *aerobic* activities.

Isometric Activities

Although isometrics do not provide much in the way of improvement of normal range of motion and endurance, they are most useful in increasing strength and volume of muscles. In isometrics, the muscle is contracted, but the length of the muscle is generally the same during contraction as during relaxation. The contraction is accomplished by keeping two joints rigid while at the same time contracting the muscle(s) between the joints. A maximum amount of force is applied against a fixed resistance during one all-out effort. An example of this is pushing or pulling against an immovable object. Let us say that if you place your hands against a wall and push with as much force as possible, you will have effected the contraction of certain muscles while their length has remained essentially the same.

Physical Activities for Children in Stressful Situations

I will close this section by presenting a set of exercises that can be used by children in stressful situations. These exercises can be particularly useful for teachers when there is stress in the school environment. The following isometrics are recommended and certainly creative adults will be able to think of others. (For these activities, muscle contraction is held for 4 or 5 seconds and then released.)

- **Hand and head press.** Interweave fingers and place hands at the back of the head with elbows pointing out. Push your head backward on the hands while simultaneously pulling the head forward with the hands. This can be done while standing or sitting at a desk.

- **Wall press.** Stand with your back against the wall. Allow the arms to hang down at the sides. Turn your hands toward the wall and press the wall with the palms, keeping the arms straight.

- **Hand pull.** Bend your right elbow and bring the right hand in with the palm close to the front of the body. Put the left hand in the right hand. Try to curl the right arm upward while simultaneously resisting with the left hand. Repeat using the opposite pressure. This can be done while standing or sitting at a desk.

- **Hand push.** Clasp your hands palms together close to your chest with the elbows pointing out. Press your hands together firmly.

- **Leg press.** While sitting at a desk or table, cross your left ankle over the right ankle. Your feet are on the floor and the legs are at about a right angle. Try to straighten your right leg while resisting with your left leg. Repeat with the right ankle over the left ankle.

- **The gripper.** Place one hand in the other and grip hard. Another variation is to grip an object. While standing, this could be the back of a chair or, while sitting, it could be the arms of the chair or seat.

- **Chair push.** While sitting at a desk or table with your hands on the armrests of the chair, push down with your hands. The entire buttocks can be raised from the chair seat. One or both feet can be lifted off the floor, or both can remain in contact with the floor.

- **Hip lifter.** While sitting at a desk or table, lift one buttock after the other from the chair seat. Try to keep your head from moving. Place your hands at the sides of the chair seat for balance.

- **Heel and toe.** From a standing position, rise up on your toes. Come back down on your heels while raising both the toes and balls of your feet.

- **Fist clencher.** Clench fists and then open your hands, extending the fingers as far as possible.

Chapter 5
Relaxation

Most of us need some type of relaxation to relieve the tensions we encounter in daily living. This chapter explores relaxation, together with the conditions that produce a relaxed state. There are many procedures that can improve our ability to relax, and we should keep in mind that what might be satisfactory for one person may not be as satisfactory for another.

When muscle fibers contract, they are responding to the electrical stimulation of impulses carried via the motor nerves. Relaxation results when this stimulation is removed. Generally speaking, there are two broad aspects of relaxation: release of muscular tension and mental diversion.

Using Relaxation with Children

Until recently, the use of relaxation to reduce stress was reserved for adults only. In more modern times, however, relaxation procedures have been found to be effective with children [Armstrong et al. 1987], and research evaluating the effectiveness of relaxation training with children has been more extensive in recent years. This research has employed a wide variety of methods and has been applied to both generalized stress disorders and specific stress responses of children. Specifically, such research has been particularly important in the areas of hyperactivity, attention and learning problems, avoidance behavior, and miscellaneous medical applications.

- **Hyperactivity.** Studies using relaxation training with hyperactive children indicate a reduction in muscle tension and improved ratings of behavior when compared to hyperactive controls [Armstrong et al. 1987]. This might suggest that such training may be an effective treatment for hyperactivity. Relaxation training, however, has not yet been proven to be superior to other treatments.

- **Learning and attention problems.** Relaxation training has also been used to treat various learning and attention problems. Children who are tense or upset often have difficulty attending to learning tasks and may be more easily frustrated or provoked than nontense children. Children taught to relax can become more amenable to learning alternative behaviors or new information. While using relaxation training for learning and attention problems has had mixed results, such training does not result in behavior that was worse than that of a control group, so training does not seem to represent a risk to test subjects. (These studies use multiple sessions of relaxation training, which strengthen the contention that repeated training is necessary for acquisition of the relaxation skill and generalization of the skill to the academic environment.)

- **Avoidance problems.** Anxiety and fear are emotions that help a person avoid engaging in an aversive activity or coming into contact with an aversive stimulus. Relaxation training has long been applied to these problems under the assumption that relaxation serves as a competing response to the undesired arousal. In addition, relaxation may also facilitate the performance of a more adaptive behavior in a stressful situation.

- **Medical problems.** Relaxation training has been increasingly applied to medical problems that are thought to be the result of or maintained by specific tension or physiological arousal [Humphrey 1989]. As such, relaxation is considered a primary treatment used to target a specific kind of medical problem. The application of relaxation training to medical problems of children seems promising. With few exceptions, the results in this area indicate that relaxation training results in symptom improvement for asthma, headaches, seizures, and insomnia, although the clinical significance of these improvements is unclear.

The Relaxation Response

The term "relaxation response" was introduced to the literature about 20 years ago by Dr. Herbert Benson of Harvard University [Benson 1975]. The "response" includes a number of body changes that occur when you experience deep muscle relaxation. The rest of this chapter introduces three relaxation techniques: progressive relaxation, meditation, and biofeedback. All of these techniques are concerned with mind-body interactions, and all are designed to induce the relaxation response.

In progressive relaxation, it is theorized that if the muscles of the body are relaxed, the mind in turn will quiet. The theory involved in meditation is that if the mind is quieted, then other systems of the body will become stabilized. Biofeedback involves the integration of progressive relaxation and meditation. Practitioners believe that the brain has the potential for voluntary control over all the systems it monitors, and that it is affected by all these systems. Thus, the intimacy of interaction between mind and body provides the mechanism through which we can learn voluntary control over biological activity.

Progressive Relaxation

Dr. Edmund Jacobson developed the technique of progressive relaxation more than 50 years ago [Jacobson 1962]. It is still the technique most often referred to in the literature and probably the one that has had the most widespread application. In this technique, the person concentrates on progressively relaxing one muscle group after another. The technique is based on the procedure of comparing the difference between tension and relaxation. That is, you sense the feeling of tension in order to get the feeling of relaxation.

Although progressive relaxation is likely to be most useful for adults, with certain variations it can be used successfully with children. For example, two of my collaborators on a childhood stress project, Dr. John Carter and Dr. Harold Russell, have developed a series of tapes for child relaxation [Carter & Russell 1984]. One of these is patterned after the idea of progressive relaxation and involves tensing and relaxing various muscle groups. This is to help make the children aware of their own muscular tension and to learn how it feels to release that tension. In the following sequence, children are asked to tense for 5 seconds and then to relax and feel the tension leaving for 10 seconds:

> Squeeze your eyes shut, tightly—hold it, relax.
> Push your lips together, tightly—hold it, relax.
> Press your tongue to the roof of your mouth—hold, relax.
> Shrug your shoulders up toward your ears—hold it, relax, feel the tension leaving.
> With both hands make a fist as tight as you can—feel the tension building—relax. Feel the tension leaving.
> Make a fist with your right hand. Notice the difference between your tense right hand and your relaxed left. Relax your right hand.
> Make a fist with your left hand. Feel the left hand getting tense while your right hand is relaxing—relax your left hand.
> Pull your stomach way in toward your backbone—hold it, relax, feel the tension leaving.
> Push your knees together hard—hold it, relax.
> Pull your toes toward your knees, way up. Hold it, hold it, relax. Feel the tension leaving your legs.
> Point your toes. Hold it, relax.
> Now, tighten every muscle in your body—hold, relax your entire body. Let your entire body get very limp, relaxed, and comfortable.

When this is completed, the adult can give breathing instructions. The children are asked to breathe in through their nose and out through their mouth, naturally and rhythmically. Each time they breathe out, they are reminded to let themselves get just a little more limp, a little more relaxed, and a little more comfortable.

Meditation

The art of meditation dates back more than 2,000 years and has been associated with both religious and cultural practices. In the 1960s, individuals began using it as a route to a more natural means of living and relaxing. Today, people from all walks of life can be counted among those who practice and realize the positive effects that meditation can have upon the human mind and body.

Of the various types of meditation, transcendental meditation (TM) is by far the best known in the United States. The benefits of TM have been documented by more than 300 scientific studies [Humphrey 1982] and include such benefits as less stress and anxiety, clearer thinking and intelligence, more energy and stamina, and more happiness and self-esteem. As many as 6,000 medical doctors in the United States have learned TM, and many recommend it to their patients as a way of staying healthy and young [Seth 1989]. TM involves the repetition of a mantra (a word or specific sound) for 15 to 20 minutes daily, while the meditator sits in a relaxed position with closed eyes.

The essential key to successful meditation is concentration. By focusing on one specific thing, such as an object or a personal feeling, it is less likely that your thoughts will be distracted. A person might want to consider focusing on such things as a fantasy trip, re-experiencing a trip already taken, a place that has not been visited, or a certain sound or chant. The importance of natural breathing rhythm should not be underestimated. In fact, some clinical psychologists recommend this as a means of concentrating. That is, you can count the number of times you inhale or exhale, and this in itself is a relaxing mental activity.

Almost without exception, those who have practiced TM attest to its positive effects. While other forms of meditation may have specific procedures, it is safe to say that most derive in some way from basic TM.

There have been countless positive pronouncements about meditation from some of the most notable scientists of modern times, who spend a good portion of their time studying stress. Only recently, however, has the scientific community uncovered many of the positive effects that the repeated practice of meditation has upon those who are stress ridden. Various scientific studies have shown that meditation can actually decrease the possibilities of an individual contracting stress-related disorders, and that meditators have a much faster recovery rate when exposed to a stressful situation than nonmeditators. Specifically, research has found that meditation decreases the body's metabolic rate, with corresponding decreases in oxygen consumption, breathing rate, heart rate and blood pressure, sympathetic nervous system activity, and blood lactate (a chemical produced in the body during stressful encounters) [Pelletier 1977].

Meditation for Children

Evidence supports the idea that the practice of meditation can be beneficial for children. All family members can learn meditation techniques, and children as young as 10 years of age can learn, although they meditate for less than 15 minutes. Often, young children become interested in learning to meditate after others in the family have begun practicing the technique.

In recent years, research on the use of meditation with children has shown that this practice can benefit them in various ways [Humphrey 1988]:

- The use of TM has been found to increase creativity, decrease anxiety, and control stress.

- Studies on child attention and meditation have shown that the attention span can be increased in children as low as kindergarten age.

- With some children, it has been found that meditation can help them to resolve certain personal problems.

- Meditating children have faster simple reaction time than nonmeditators. (Simple reaction time is the amount of time it takes from the time a signal is given until the initial movement.)

- Child meditators demonstrate greater eye-hand coordination and handle tasks faster and more accurately than nonmeditators. If there is any credence to the theory that improved perceptual-motor performance results in improved academic achievement, then the value of meditation in this connection is readily discerned. It should be mentioned, however, that research does not conclusively support the idea that improved perceptual-motor performance will always result in better academic achievement. Some studies tend to support the theory, others do not. Nevertheless, the use of meditation in this area should continue to be explored.

- With reference to exceptional children, meditation is important to special education, since it is purported to improve learning, memory, grades, interpersonal relationships, and cognitive perceptual functioning. Thus, meditation would be applicable to exceptional or developmentally disabled children.

Biofeedback

The term feedback has been used in various frames of reference. It may have been used originally in engineering in connection with control systems that involve feedback procedures. These feedback control systems make adjustments to environmental changes. (An example is the thermostat that controls temperature levels in your home.)

Researchers estimate that there are perhaps millions of individual feedback systems in the human body. Our five senses receive information about the external environment and relay that information to a control center, usually the brain, where it is integrated with other relevant information. When the sensed information is significant enough, central control generates commands for appropriate changes. Some examples of feedback control systems are scratching an itch, hitting a tennis ball with a racquet, pupil accommodation for near and far vision, perspiration, sneezing, sleeping, urinating, and eating.

The human body itself is a complicated and complex biofeedback instrument that alerts us to certain internal activity. Many students of the subject feel, however, that there is still a need for sensitive instruments to monitor physiological and psychological reactivity. Following is a brief discussion of some of the more widely known biofeedback instruments that are used for both research and therapeutic purposes.

- **Electromyograph.** Electromyography (EMG) is the recording of electric activity that occurs in muscles during contraction. Needle or skin electrodes record these activities, which can be recorded on an *oscilloscope*. This procedure helps to determine what muscles, or even parts of muscles, participate in movement. When a muscle is completely relaxed or inactive, it has no electrical activity. When it is contracted, indications of electric activity appear. Practitioners believe that EMG training can produce deep muscle relaxation and thus, relieve tension. A person gets feedback by watching a dial or hearing a sound from the machine, and thus he knows immediately the extent to which certain muscles are tensed or relaxed. (A muscle frequently used in EMG training for research and other purposes is the *frontalis*, located in the front of the head.) EMG is effective in retraining a person following an injury or disease, because the recording of electric activity can show the individual small increments of gain in function of a muscle. (Incidentally, this instrument is the one most frequently used in biofeedback research with children.)

- **Feedback thermometers**. The obvious purpose of feedback thermometers is to record body temperature. Ordinarily, a *thermistor* is attached to the hands or the fingers. This highly sensitive instrument shows small increments in degrees of temperature change, so that the person receives the information with a visual or auditory signal. This kind of feedback instrumentation has been recommended for such purposes as reduction of stress and anxiety and for autonomic nervous system relaxation.

- **Electroencephalograph**. The purpose of the electroencephalograph (EEG) is to record amplitude and frequency of brainwaves, and it has been used in research for many years. The EEG has also been used with success to diagnose certain clinical diseases. In addition, feedback EEG has found use in psychotherapy and in stress and pain reduction.

- **Galvanic skin response**. There are several different kinds of galvanic skin response (GSR) instruments used to measure changes in electrical resistance of the skin. These changes indicate emotional arousal. The instrument responds to the amount of perspiration that is emitted, and the person perceives the change in electrical resistance through an auditory or visual signal. GSR feedback is often recommended for use in relaxation, reducing tension, improvement of ability to sleep, and for emotional control.

In general, the purpose of biofeedback machinery is to provide accurate and reliable data that will increase a person's awareness of how her or his body is functioning, and to demonstrate the influence on his or her reactions of the body. Hopefully, this information should be useful in inspiring a person to take an active self-interest in his or her own well-being. After such information is received, if it has been obtained under the supervision of a qualified therapist, the therapist can arrange a given number of sessions for consultation and training. Perhaps the ultimate objective is for the individual to be able to gain control over his or her own autonomic nervous system.

Biofeedback for Children

Biofeedback has been used with considerable success with children, and research in the use of biofeedback with children has increased appreciably in recent years. Following is a summary of representative findings of this research [Rosenbaum 1989]:

- Children who are not aware of their own tensed state can benefit from biofeedback training.

- Biofeedback-induced relaxation can assist children with learning disabilities in reaching their educational potentials.

- EMG training can be useful in the treatment of hyperactivity in children.

- EMG training has been shown to increase attention to an academic task as well as reducing problem behavior.

Most experts in the field of biofeedback believe that such treatment can provide possibilities for increased functioning and self-regulation of body and mind in children.

Notes

Armstrong, F. D. (1987). Relaxation training with children: A review of the literature. In J. H. Humphrey (Ed.), *Human stress: Current selected research* (Vol. 2). New York: AMS Press, Inc.

Benson, H. (1975). *The relaxation response.* New York: William Morrow and Co., Inc.

Carter, J. L., & Russell, H. L. (1984). Use of biofeedback relaxation procedures with learning disabled children. In J. H. Humphrey (Ed.), *Stress in childhood*. New York: AMS Press, Inc.

Humphrey, J. H. (1982). *A textbook of stress*. Springfield, IL: Charles C Thomas Publisher.

Humphrey, J. H. (1988). *Children and stress*. New York: AMS Press, Inc.

Humphrey, J. H. (1989). A review of some recent research on stress and children with an affliction. In J. H. Humphrey (Ed.), *Human stress: Current selected research* (Vol. 3). New York: AMS Press, Inc.

Jacobson, E. (1962). *You must relax* (4th ed.). New York: McGraw-Hill Book Co.

Pelletier, K. R. (1977). *Mind as healer mind as slayer*. New York: Dell Publishing Co., Inc.

Rosenbaum, L. (1989). Biofeedback frontiers. In J. H. Humphrey (Ed.), *Stress in modern society* (No. 15). New York: AMS Press, Inc.

Sethi, A. S. (1989). Meditation as an intervention in stress reactivity. In J. H. Humphrey (Ed.), *Stress in modern society* (No. 12). New York: AMS Press, Inc.

Chapter 6
Stunt Games

In stunt games, caregivers use stories to encourage children to imitate animals, elements of nature, or other people through activities that require balance, coordination, flexibility, agility, and strength. This chapter provides several such stories, whose activities in one way or another involve contracting the muscles in tensing-relaxing movements. Caregivers can read the stories to children, or, depending upon their reading level, the children can read the stories themselves. This chapter presents the story, provides a description of the activity depicted in the story, and then offers a suggested application. (These stunt games can be used with an individual child or with a group of children.)

It is entirely possible that some adults will want to develop some of their own stunt games, and I heartily recommend that they try their hand at it. Following are some guidelines for consideration:

- In general, the new wordload should be kept relatively low.

- When new words are used, there should be as much repetition of these words as is possible and appropriate.

- Consider sentence length and avoid complex sentences to keep the difficulty of the material within the ability level of children.

- Also consider the reading values and literary merits of a story. Using a character in a story setting helps to develop interest.

- The activity to be used in the stunt game story should not be readily identifiable. When children identify an activity early in the story, they may pay little attention to getting the details they need to engage in the experience.

Franky Frog Jumps

Franky Frog sits.
He is ready.
He jumps.
Sit like Franky.
Jump like Franky.

The child squats down on feet and hands, jumps off the floor by springing into the air from both feet and hands, then lands on feet and hands.

Engage the children in a discussion of frogs and how they move. The discussion can focus on how a frog sits and then suddenly jumps. Body tension occurs when the frog (child) is preparing to jump, as well as during the jump. Tension is released at the end of the jump.

Willie Worm

I move like Willie Worm.
I move in front.
I move in back.
I move along.
I will stop quickly.

The child lies face down on the floor, pushes up, and places his weight on his hands and toes. He keeps his elbows straight and body stiff. He brings his feet up close to his hands by walking while he keeps his hands in place. Then, keeping his feet in place, he walks on the hands until his body is extended again. He continues in this manner.

Start a discussion about how a worm moves. Then ask the children how they might do this. The body tenses as the child prepares to move like a worm. The tensed muscle relaxes as the adult gives a signal to stop quickly.

Jumping Jack

I am a jumping jack.
I jump way up.
I jump way down.
I will jump up and down.

The child squats down low in a crouched position and exerts energy by jumping up. The child lands lightly on the feet and then falls to the floor. (Most activities that require landing should be performed on a soft landing surface, such as a carpet or matting.)

Lead a discussion of how a jack-in-the-box functions. A child can then try to do this. Tension occurs during preparation for the jump and during the jump.

Curly Cat Takes a Walk

Curly Cat is asleep.
Curly Cat opens his eyes.
Curly Cat takes a walk.
He walks with long steps.
He holds his head high.
He walks around.
Try to walk like Curly Cat.
Put your hands on the floor.
Walk all around like Curly Cat.

The child walks on the hands and feet while arching the back.

Start a discussion about cats as pets. Ask what a cat does when it wakes up. Tension occurs as the child assumes the position to walk, and it also occurs during the walk. The muscles relax when the "cat" stops and lies down.

George Giraffe

There is a tall animal in a faraway land.
He has a long neck.
His name is George Giraffe.
You could look like him if you did this.
Place your arms high over your head.
Put your hands together.
Point them to the front.
This will be his neck and head.
Now walk like George Giraffe.
This is how.
Stand on your toes.
Walk with your legs straight.

The child stands straight with arms extended upward, then bends the wrists forward with fingers pointing straight ahead and the thumbs interlocked. The child walks with legs stiff.

Ask who has been to a zoo. Focus on the kinds of animals in the zoo and guide the discussion so that children start thinking about giraffes. (It is also useful to begin the discussion with a picture of a giraffe.) Muscle tension occurs when the child assumes the position for the giraffe walk and then actually walks. As in the case of the previous activity (cat walk), the adult may give a signal for the giraffe to drop to the floor. This provides for muscular relaxation.

The Jumping Rabbit

I can jump like a rabbit.
I can sit like a rabbit.
I put my hands on the floor.
Now I jump.
My feet come up to my hands.
I hold my hands in front.
I put my hands on the floor.
I jump again and again.
On the last jump I will fall down.

The child squats, places the hands on the floor in front, and jumps with both feet to bring them up close to the hands. The child can place the hands in front again and make several jumps in this manner.

Engage the children in any type of discussion that involves rabbits and their habits. In this discussion, consider how rabbits move. There is tension in the preparation for the jump and the jump itself. There is relaxation when the rabbit falls over on the last jump.

Casper Camel

Casper Camel lives in the zoo.
He has a hump on his back.
Could you look like Casper Camel?
You will need a hump.
Try it this way.
Bend forward.
Put your arms behind your back.
Hold them together.

The child stands straight and places the hands behind the back and folds them. Next, the child bends forward at the waist and tries to raise the arms in the back. The child walks, swinging from side to side.

This will be a hump.
That will look like Casper Camel.
Take a step.
Lift your head.
Take a step.
Lift your head.
Move like Casper Camel.

Before reading the story, lead a discussion on camels and how they walk. It might be a good idea to show a picture of a camel. Tension of the muscles of the trunk occurs when the child is preparing for the camel walk and when the movement is actually executed. After the child performs the activity for a short time, call for the camel to fall and this action releases tension.

The Clowns Do a Stunt

Have you ever seen clowns at a circus?
Sometimes they do funny things.
Once I saw two clowns
   do a stunt together.
This is what they did.
They sat back to back.
Their feet were flat on the floor.
Their feet were close to their bodies.
They locked their arms together.
They pushed their back together.
They pushed hard.
As they pushed they began to rise.
At last they were standing.
They sat down and did the stunt again.
Could you do this stunt with a friend?

This activity requires two children of about equal size who push hard against the other to rise to the standing position.

Introduce a conversation about the clowns and the many things they do to make people laugh. Read the story and encourage the children to experiment with the stunt. A great deal of tension occurs when they try to rise to a standing position, and it is relieved when they reach this position.

Circus Elephant

I saw the circus.
I saw many animals.
I saw an elephant.
He was big.
He had big legs.
He had a trunk.
He swings his trunk.
I will walk like the elephant.

The child bends forward at the waist with knees straight, holds the arms straight down in front, and clasps the hands. The child then walks slowly without bending the knees while swinging the arms from side to side.

Begin a discussion on circus elephants and how they move and what they do in the circus. There is tension in the muscles of the trunk as the child walks with legs and arms stiff. To release the tension, give a signal for the elephant to fall down.

Tick, Tock

Listen to the clock.
It says, "Tick, tock" as it keeps the time.
Would you like to play you are a clock?
This is the way.
Stand up.
Keep your arms straight.
Now keep time with the clock by
    moving your arms.
Ready.

In this activity a child pretends to be a clock and uses the arms as the hands of the clock, moving the arms as the adult recites the verse.

Move your arms like a clock.
Keep your arms stiff and straight.
Here are some words to say to the "tick, tock" of the clock.
    Tick, tock, tick, tock.
    Be bright and gay.
    It's time to start another day.
    Tick, tock, tick, tock.
    Tick, tock, tick, tock.
    Oh! Let's stop the clock.

Begin a discussion about clocks and about why we need them. Ask the child to pretend to be a clock and think about the hands of the clock. The arm muscles are tensed as the child moves them like the hands of a clock. When the clock stops, the child drops the arms and relaxes.

Push the Wheelbarrow

Have you ever seen a wheelbarrow go?
You can play you are a wheelbarrow.
You will need a friend to play with you.
You can be the wheelbarrow.
You get down on your hands and knees.
Your hands will be the wheel.
You walk along on your hands.
Your friend steers the wheelbarrow.
Whoops! The wheelbarrow breaks down.
Now your friend can be the wheelbarrow.
You can steer the wheelbarrow.
Oh! Oh! The wheelbarrow breaks down again.

> _The children take a partner of about equal size and strength. One child lies down with the hands on the floor, elbows straight, and extends the feet behind him. The other child carries the feet of the first child, who keeps the knees straight. The child becomes a wheelbarrow by walking on the hands. Children change positions so that each can be the wheelbarrow._

Lead a discussion about wheelbarrows, including what they are, how they run, and what can be done with them. Ask the children to think of ways that they could be wheelbarrows. When the activity is performed, the child who is the wheelbarrow experiences a great deal of tension in the arms. There is relaxation when the wheelbarrow breaks down.

Airplanes Go

I look up.
I hold my arms out.
I am an airplane.

In this activity, the child pretends to be an airplane, using the arms as the wings of the plane.

My arms are the wings.
They are stiff.
I go round and round.
I stop.

Any discussion about airplanes is a lively one, and children like to pretend to be an airplane. Emphasize the importance of the wings and how strong they must be. This tends to prompt the child to hold the arms out straight and stiff. Relaxation occurs when the airplane stops.

Sally Seal

A seal lives in the sea.
Sometimes it lives in the zoo.
There is one in the zoo called
   Sally Seal.
She likes to swim.
She can also walk on land.
Would you like to try to walk like Sally Seal?
Try it this way.
Put your hands on the floor.
Put your feet back.
put your weight on your hands and on top of your toes.
Now walk on your hands and drag your legs.
Sally Seal gets tired and falls down.

The child moves on the hands, holds the legs rigid, and drags them behind.

The discussion can focus on seals, especially their habits and the different ways they can move. Many children will have seen them on television, if not in real life at the circus or the zoo. One of the things that children tend to remember about seals is the way they can balance and the sounds they make. Although this activity places some tension on the arms, there is also a great deal of muscular rigidity in the legs. Emphasize keeping the legs as stiff as possible as the seal walks. This tension is released when the seal falls down.

Chapter 7
Creative Movement

Creative experience involves self-expression and responds to children's need to experiment, to express original ideas, and to think. Creativity and childhood enjoy a congruous relationship, because children are naturally creative. They imagine. They pretend. They are uninhibited. They are not only original but actually ingenious in their thoughts and actions. Indeed, creativity is a characteristic inherent in the lives of practically all children and may range from some children who create as a natural form of expression without adult stimulation to others who may need varying degrees of adult guidance and encouragement.

Traditional approaches to creative expression include art, music, and writing. The essence of creative expression, however, is movement. Movement, as a form of creativity, uses the body as the instrument of expression. For the young child, the most natural form of creative expression is movement. Children have a natural inclination for movement, and they use this medium as their basic form of creative expression. Movement is the child's language, a most important form of communication, and a most meaningful way of learning.

Relaxation Through Creative Movement

Relaxation through creative movement combines a form of imagery and tensing and releasing. (Imagery will be discussed in detail in the following chapter.) A child or group of children with various degrees of adult guidance creates a movement designed to tense and relax individual muscles, muscle groups, or the entire body. When this involves an individual muscle or a group of muscles, it can be called specific relaxation, and when it involves the entire body, it can be referred to as general relaxation. The procedure is applicable in either the school or home setting. Whether used with one child or several children, the procedures are essentially the same.

Following is an example that shows the contrast (tensing and letting go) of the muscles of the arm.

> Ask a question, such as "What would you say is the main difference between a baseball bat and a jump rope?" The discussion will no doubt lead to the major difference being that a baseball bat is hard and stiff and that a jump rope is soft and limp. The adult might then proceed as follows:
>
> Let's see if we can make one of our arms be like a bat. (Children create this movement.) Now quickly, can you make your arm be like a jump rope? (Children create the movement by releasing the tensed arm.)

You can then evaluate the experience with such questions as: How did your arm feel when you made it like a bat? How did your arm feel when you made it like a jump rope?

The creative adult and the children can talk together about the relaxation phenomenon. This is but one approach, and adults are limited only by their own creativity and imagination.

Creative Movements for General Relaxation

This section examines creative movements designed to relax the entire body (general); later sections will focus on creative movements for particular muscles or muscle groups (specific). As you consider these recommended creative movement experiences, keep the following general suggestions in mind.

- **Because of their nature, most creative movement experiences tend to be relaxing.** The reason for this is that they are conducted in an informal atmosphere with a minimum amount of formal structuring.

- **Although most children are naturally creative, some will manifest more creativity than others.** This means that, depending upon the nature of a particular creative experience, along with the creative level of a child, the adult needs to determine the amount of guidance needed in each situation. With practice, most adults will be able to make a judgment that is in the best interest of the children.

- **The manner in which an adult speaks, along with the intonation of certain words, can have a profound influence on children's creative responses.** For example, a soft tone of voice tends to make children respond with a slower movement. A sharp or loud tone tends to cause children to respond more vigorously. Even the words can have an influence on children's responses. For instance, words like hard and soft and heavy and light are likely to inspire feelings and emotions that will result in varying responses. The important thing to keep in mind is that there should be a contrasting experience—tensing and letting go. The voice can have a profound influence on this experience.

- **The format for conducting the various activities is intended only as a general way of organizing the experiences.** For this reason, the suggested procedures should be considered as a guide and not necessarily as a prescription to be followed. In other words, individuals should inject their own creative ideas into the procedures for conducting the experiences. The format I suggest here consists of the name of the activity, suggested adult input, some possible children's responses, and suggested evaluation questions.

- **The questions of where to conduct the activities is important.** Some can be conducted while sitting in a chair or on the floor. Others may require more space. The nature of the activity itself will ordinary indicate where the activity might best take place. One important consideration in this regard is that, for those activities where the child might respond by falling to the floor, a soft landing surface should be provided, such as a rug or other suitable soft landing surface.

Children's creative movement responses are pretty much an individual matter; that is, each child is likely to respond in the way that the experience means to him or her personally. Therefore, a creative movement experience can be conducted with a group of children, and each child will create his or her unique response. At the same time, any of the recommended activities can be used with a single child.

Hard and Soft

The major purpose of this activity is to help the child distinguish between the terms hard and soft.

Ask the children if they know the difference between hard and soft. Children might respond by naming some things that are hard or soft. If this does not happen, guide the discussion with certain questions:

- Is a rock hard?

- Can you make a rock soft?

- Is the pavement hard?

- Can it be made soft?

(The purpose here is to help those children who do not know the difference, or how to explain the difference, to distinguish between hard and soft. All such questions will be governed by the original responses of children.)

Adult: We have talked about some of the things that are hard and some that are soft. Now, I wonder if you could do something to make yourself hard?

Children respond by creating shapes and positions that depict their bodies as being hard.

Adult: Now, can you do something that will make your body feel soft?

Children do several things that give them the feeling of a soft body.

Adult: All right. Very good. I am going to say the word "hard" and when you hear it, I want you to make yourself feel hard. After that, I will say the word "soft" and then you make yourself feel soft.

Call out the word "hard" and have the children hold their position for 3 or 4 seconds before calling out the word "soft." Continue using the words "harder" and "hardest" and "softer" and "softest." Take advantage of appropriate intonation of the words "hard" and "soft."

Start a discussion with such questions as the following:

- How did you feel when you were hard?

- How did you feel when you were soft?

- Did you feel better when you pretended you were hard or when you were soft?

- Could you feel the difference?

Cold and Hot

In working with children in creative movement, I have found that there are certain conditions that cause children to react more or less "naturally" to specific situations. The activity "Cold and Hot" is a case in point. When children are asked to respond to "cold," they tend to react with a "tensed up" body condition. When responding to "hot," they react with a more relaxed state. This is probably because children have had the actual experience of being cold and hot.

Introduce the discussion by referring to certain climatic or seasonal conditions that will depict cold and hot.

- Is a piece of ice hot or cold?

- Is the sun hot or cold?

- If you have been out on a winter day, how did it make you feel?

- How does it feel to be out on a summer day?

- Can you think of some things that are cold or hot?

Guide the discussion in the direction of how a child feels when the body is cold and/or hot. Some children are likely to suggest that they shiver when cold and sweat when hot. Others will tell about their experiences with things that are hot and cold.

Adult: You have told a lot of things about cold and hot. Now, how would you like to show how it feels to be cold and how it feels to be hot? When I say the word "cold," please show what you would do with your body. When I say the word "hot," show what your body would do.

Continue with this procedure as the children create body movements that express hot and cold.

Adult: Did you feel "looser" when you were cold or when you were hot? George, you made your body into a ball when I said "cold," and when I said "hot," you flopped over and spread out your arms. Why did you do that? Could you tell us the different feeling you had when you pretended to be cold than when you pretended to be hot?

Rain and Snow

It has been my experience that when children are asked to imitate rain, they tend to make their bodies tense. When imitating snow, they appear to relax the body. I have speculated that the reason for this is that they generally associate rain as heavy and snow as light. Some adults may try to guide the discussion in this particular direction. One good way to introduce this activity is to ask what the difference is between rain and snow.

Some typical responses are the following:

- Rain is wetter than snow.

- Rain comes down harder than snow.

- Snow is white; rain does not have a color.

- It is more fun playing in the snow than it is in the rain.

- My mother doesn't care if I play in the snow, but she does not like to have me play in the rain.

Adult: You have suggested some interesting ways in which snow and rain are different. Now, how do you think it would make you feel to pretend you are rain—and then snow?

Children express different feelings.

Adult: You have told many different ways it could feel to be like rain and snow. Now, pretend that you are one and then the other. I will say "rain," and then I will say "snow."

Alternate calling out "rain" and "snow" as the children create movements in the form of these two elements.

Adult: Which did you like best—pretending you were rain or pretending you were snow?
How did it feel to be rain?
How did it feel to be snow?
When did it feel more restful—when you were rain or when you were snow?
Did you feel heavier when you were rain?
Did you feel heavier when you were snow?
Which one gave you a better feeling?

Peanut Butter and Milk

This activity is similar to the preceding one, because the substances (peanut butter and milk) have contrasting consistencies. Peanut butter is a thick substance, while milk is thin.

Introduce the discussion by raising questions about the two foods, as follows:

- How many of you drink milk every day?

- How many of you have eaten peanut butter?

- What is the difference between the two?

- What do you think would happen if we tried to pour peanut butter like we pour milk?

Children generally respond in terms of the thickness of peanut butter and the thinness of milk. Typical responses are the following:

- You don't spread milk like you do peanut butter.

- You can't make a sandwich out of milk.

- You eat peanut butter, but you drink milk.

- You can eat a peanut butter sandwich, and then drink milk.

Adult: Those are all good ideas. Now, how do you think it would feel to make your body like peanut butter and then like milk? Let's try it. I will say "peanut butter," and then I will say "milk," and you try to change from one to the other.

Adult: How did you feel when you made yourself like peanut butter?
How did you feel when you made yourself like milk?
Was it easier to make yourself like peanut butter or like milk?
Which was more fun?

The Kite

This activity elicits movement imitating a kite in flight being kept up by the wind, which is compared to moving like a kite when the wind ceases and the kite begins to descend.
Pose questions such as the following:

- What is a kite?

- How many of you have ever had a kite?

- Did you ever try to make a kite fly?

- How can you make a kite fly?

- What makes a kite stay in the air?

- What happens when a kite begins to fall?

There will be many various responses. Guide the discussion in the direction of the purpose of the activity.

Adult: How do you think it would feel to be like a kite up in the air?

Children express their feelings, and the adult encourages them to demonstrate. Children will perform in many different ways, but the most prevalent way is taking a forward leaning stance with arms outspread to the side. This tends to cause the muscles of the body to become tense.

Adult: You are all very good at being a kite. Now, let's try being a kite in the air, kept up by the wind, and a kite after the wind stops blowing. When I say "up," it will mean that you are a kite in the air, and when I say "down" it will mean that the wind has stopped and the kite comes down.

Adult: How did you feel when you were a kite in the air?
How did you feel when the wind stopped?
What was the difference in your body when you were a kite in the air and when you were a kite when the wind stopped?

The Balloon

This activity challenges the children to move like a balloon when it is blown up to capacity and then when the air is suddenly released. An important feature of this activity is that it helps a child learn about controlled breathing, which is so important to muscular relaxation. This activity provides for rhythm in breathing as the child inhales deeply, then exhales, and becomes relaxed when the air is released from the balloon.

Introduce this activity with questions like the following:

- Did you ever blow up a balloon and then let it go?

- What happens if you blow too hard?

- What happens if you let it go?

Start the discussion with a real balloon—blow it up and then let go. Proceed with the questions and the discussion.

Children will provide many responses verbally, but many times they will immediately try to show what a balloon does when it is let go with air in it.

Adult: Good! You are acting like you are a balloon. Now, let's blow up like a balloon, and when I say "let go," do what a balloon would do when the air comes out.

Adult: Did you feel tight when you took the air in like a balloon?
How did it make you feel when you were holding the air?
How did it make you feel when you let go?
Was it a better feeling to hold the air in or to let it go?

Creative Movements for Specific Relaxation

Most of the procedures recommended in the preceding section of the chapter apply in this section as well. The creative movements in this section, however, are organized under the headings of specific muscle groups:

- Muscles of the head, face, tongue, and neck;

- Muscles of the trunk;

- Muscles of the arms; and

- Muscles of the legs.

A number of the muscles in the trunk may be grouped with the muscles of the arms, since the trunk muscles attach the upper limbs to the torso and move the shoulders and arms. This means that there can be some overlapping from one muscle group to another. Notice that some of the activities involve a certain degree of structuring. This means that, while a child should still be free to explore various ways of performing an activity, the adult provides enough guidance in the creative response to direct the activity.

Muscles of the Head, Face, Tongue, and Neck

Children particularly enjoy activities in this muscle group, because it gives them an opportunity to make funny faces.

Big Eye

In this activity, children open their eyes as wide as possible for a period of about 4 to 5 seconds. They can look to the right, left, above, and below.

Name the activity and ask the children what they think it means. Some children will immediately respond by opening their eyes wide.

Adult: When I say "big eye," try to open your eyes wide and hold it until I say "little eye."

Adult: How did it feel to have a big eye?
Did it feel different to have a little eye?

The Sneeze

The muscles are contracted on either side of the nose as in sneezing. The skin should be wrinkled upward over the nose as hard as possible. Introduce the activity by discussing how you look when you sneeze. (You can also discuss what causes you to sneeze.)

Children find this a funny activity, and they will respond in a variety of ways. Some of them will immediately try to do a forced sneeze.

Adult: Show how you would look when you are getting ready to sneeze. When I say "ready" pretend to get ready to sneeze. When I say "sneeze," pretend to sneeze.

Adult: Did your face feel tight when you were getting ready to sneeze?
How did your face feel after you pretended to sneeze?

Rabbit Nose

In this activity, the children dilate and flare their nostrils. Introduce the discussion by considering how rabbits move, the color of their fur, and other features.

Some children will have either had a pet rabbit or will have seen one in a pet store. They are willing to tell many things that they know about them, because rabbits are a favorite with children.

Adult: (If none of the children respond about the quick movements that a rabbit makes with its nose, point the discussion in this direction.)

Have you ever noticed how rabbits make their noses move out and in? I wonder why they do this? Maybe you could pretend to be a rabbit and make this movement with your nose. When I say "out," pretend to make this movement with your nose. When I say "stop," let your nose change back to the way it way before.

Adult: Did your nose feel tight when you made a rabbit nose? How did it feel when you let your nose change back?

The Frown

There are many ways to perform this activity, which include stretching the left corner of the mouth up and out, stretching the right corner of the mouth down and out, stretching the left corner of the mouth down and out, and stretching the lower lip down hard while trying to keep the lip flat.

Begin a discussion about smiling and frowning, with consideration of how they are alike and different, why people smile and frown, and what it means to keep a "straight" face. Also mention the different kinds of frowns suggested above.

While children will respond verbally, more often than not, they will immediately respond by frowning and smiling.

Adult: Let's play a game in which we will use different kinds of frowns. Remember the different kinds of frowns we talked about. When I say "frown," make any kind of frown you please, and hold it until I say "straight." This means that you should quickly change from the frown to a straight face.

Adult: Was your face stiff when you frowned?
Did your face feel loose when you changed from a frown to a straight face?
What do you think happened?

The Hard Whistle

Children pretend to whistle by tensing the lips vigorously. Ask the children how many of them can whistle. Follow this with a discussion of what causes the whistling sound.

The responses can be noisy, because those children who can do so are likely to begin immediately to whistle.

Adult: Did you notice the shape of your mouth and lips? They formed a circle. Now, let's try what we will call the hard whistle. What does that suggest to you?

Children give various comments on the position of the lips in the hard whistle.

Adult: Let's try the hard whistle, when I say "whistle." When I say "stop," let your lips go back to the regular position.

Adult: What kind of feeling did you have on your mouth and lips when you did the hard whistle?
Did your lips feel tight?
How did they feel when you stopped?

The Silent Yell

In this activity, the children open their mouths wide in any direction and hold this position until the release.

Start the discussion by mentioning that children call out to each other when they are playing outside. Ask what these calls are named.

Children give these calls different names, and someone is likely to say that they are yelling. If not, mention this.

Adult: (Continue the discussion by considering why people yell, as well as the sound made by yelling. Finally, direct the discussion to the shape of the face when yelling.)

Now, let's try doing what we will call the silent yell. When I say "yell," act like you are yelling, but don't make a sound. When I say "stop," let your face return to normal.

Adult: Did your face feel stiff when you acted like you were yelling? How did it feel when you stopped?

Muscles of the Trunk

The activity in this classification is presented in the form of a creative story game, using the same format as in Chapter 6.

Row Your Boat

Adult: You will need a partner to play "Row Your Boat." Sit down facing your partner. Put your feet together. Reach out, and take hold of hands. Now you are in a boat. Pull each other back and forth to row your boat. Sing as you row. Row to the beat of the music.

Row, row, row your boat, pulling to and fro.
Happily, happily, happily, happily singing as you go.
Row, row, row your boat, up the stream you go.
Happily, happily, happily, happily singing as you go.

Two children of nearly the same size sit opposite each other and join hands. As the music is played or as they sing, they pull vigorously back and forth.

The introductory discussion can focus on boats and on what one has to do when rowing a boat. Introduce the story, and the children can then practice the song before "rowing." There is tension in the trunk muscles when rowing the boat. It is released when the song is ended or when the musical accompaniment stops. The muscles of the upper and lower extremities are also involved in this activity. Stories such as "Casper Camel" and "The Clowns Do a Stunt," which were presented in Chapter 6, can also be used for this purpose.

Muscles of the Arms

The Squeezer

This activity involves squeezing an imaginary object by making a tightly clenched fist and releasing to an open hand. Start by asking what the word "squeeze" means, how you squeeze something, and when you need to squeeze.

Children will give all sorts of responses: You squeeze lemons. You squeeze tight on a bat when you hit a ball. I like to squeeze my toothpaste. I once squeezed a cherry and a seed popped out.

Adult: There are certainly many things to squeeze and ways to squeeze them. The kind of squeeze I am thinking about is one in which you would use your whole hand to squeeze something, let's say like a small rubber ball. Let's try it.

When I say "squeeze," pretend to squeeze something in your hand. You can pretend you have something in each hand. I will say "open," and you can stop squeezing and let your hand come open.

Adult: Did your hands get tired when you squeezed hard? How did it feel when I said "open"?

The Rubber Band

One way to be like a rubber band is to clasp the hands tightly in front of the chest with the elbows pointing out to the sides and then to try as hard as possible to pull the hands apart.

Start a conversation about rubber bands and their uses. Present different-sized rubber bands to stretch to various lengths. This is exciting for the children, because they wonder if the rubber band is going to break.

Children will eagerly enter a discussion about rubber bands, because almost all of them will have had some sort of experience with them.

Adult: I wonder how it would feel to be a rubber band and stretch like one? Let's try some movements that would make us be like a rubber band.

Children do a large variety of movements depicting a rubber band.

Adult: I noticed that some of you held your hands together like your arms were a rubber band. (If this does not happen, you can suggest it.) Let's try to stretch the rubber band until it breaks. When I say "start," try to stretch hard like a rubber band. When I say "snap," pretend that the rubber bands breaks.

Adult: Did your arms get tired when you were stretching them like a rubber band?
Did your hands and arms feel tight?
How did it feel when I said "snap"?

The Weight Lifter

For this activity, the child lifts an imaginary weight, straining as if actually lifting a heavy weight. The child stands upright, with the weight on the floor in front, bends at the knees, stoops, and picks up the weight with both hands, curling it to the chest.

Ask what is meant by the term weight lifter. Since weight lifting has become a popular event, many children will have seen the activity on television. They are interested in the strength it takes to lift the heavy weights.

Adult: Focus the discussion on various ways to lift weights, with emphasis on the curl.
What do you think we mean when we say that one way of lifting a weight is the curl?

Some children will know immediately and will demonstrate why it is called the curl. (Weight is curled by the arms up to the chest.)

Adult: Let's see if we can pretend to be weight lifters and try the curl. When I say "curl," pretend you are lifting a heavy weight. When I say "stop," pretend to drop the weight.

Adult: Did your arms feel tight when you were lifting the weight?
Did your arms get a tired feeling?
How did it feel when the weight was dropped?

Muscles of the Legs

Ankle Snap

In this activity, the child flexes (bends) the ankle hard toward the body in order to stretch the muscles at the back of the legs from the knee down. The child holds this position for a short period, and then extends the foot outward for a short period. Finally, the child releases the position and relaxes the muscles. Each ankle can be flexed and extended separately.

Center the discussion around the various extremities of the body with reference to how the different kinds of joints can bend. Name the activity, and then ask the children what they think is meant by it.

The kind of introduction mentioned above will likely result in many kinds of responses indicating experiences children have had with various body joints.

Adult: (Take into account the different responses and then attempt to direct these to the activity.)

You have suggested many things that can be done with the ankles. Could you show us some of these things?

Children react with different ankle movements. If you notice a movement similar to the ankle snap, point this out.

Adult: Let's play the ankle snap game. When I say "stretch in," try to do this, and when I say "stretch out," try to do that. When I say "snap," quickly stop stretching the ankle.

Adult: Did you stretch as hard as you could?
How did it feel?
Did you feel a change when I said "snap"?
How did that feel?

Kick Up

This activity is best accomplished from a sitting position in a chair or the edge of a desk or table. Have the children sit so that the edge of the chair is under their knee, extend one leg, and hold it for a short period. The extended leg should be stiff. After the short period, the children can allow the leg to bend back to the original position. Each leg can be extended separately.

Begin by asking the children about kicking as a movement. Make particular references to the use of kicking as a skill in certain kinds of activities.

Children are likely to mention games in which the skill of kicking is used, such as football, soccer, and the popular game of kickball, played in many schools.

Adult: (After discussing kicking in general, ask about kicking from a sitting position.)

This will, of course, evoke many different reactions, because children will not likely think of kicking in this manner.

Adult: This is an activity called "Kick Up." What does that mean to you? Let's try it. When I say "kick up," will you please do so, and hold it until I say "down."

Adult: How did it feel to kick up?
Did your leg feel stiff?
Did your leg get tired when you held it up?
How did it feel when I said "down"?

All of the activities presented here have been field-tested with many children. They have met with a great deal of success as a means of relieving tension and, thus, of helping to reduce stress.

Chapter 8
Mental Practice and Imagery

Mental practice occurs when you imagine in your own mind the way to perform a given activity. Imagery is developing a mental picture that may help you perform an activity. In mental practice, you think through what you are going do, and with imagery, you or another person may suggest an image, and you then try to effect that mental picture.

The use of mental practice in performing motor skills is not new. In fact, research in this general area has been going on for more than 50 years [Koehler 1987]. This research has revealed that picturing a movement will produce recordable electric actions in the muscle groups that would be called upon if the movement is actually carried out. In addition, most mental activity is accompanied by a general rise in muscular tension.

Mental practice for relaxation involves making suggestions to yourself. For the most part, in early childhood we first learn to act on the basis of verbal instructions from others. Later we learn to guide and direct our own behavior on the basis of our own language activities—we literally talk to ourselves, giving ourselves instructions. This point of view has long been supported by research postulating that speech as a form of communication between children and adults later becomes a way for the child to organize his or her own behavior [Luria 1959]. That is, the function that was previously divided between two people—the child and the adult—becomes an internal function of the child's behavior.

An example of mental practice in relaxation would be to go through from "head to toe" as follows:

> I am going to relax completely. First, I will relax my forehead and scalp. I will let all the muscles of my forehead and scalp relax and become completely at rest. All of the wrinkles will come out of my forehead and that part of my body will relax completely. Now, I will relax the muscles of my face. I will just let them relax and go limp. (And so on from head to toe.)

For years, research studies have reported success in using imagery for relaxation with children. Some studies show that imagery can be used effectively with hyperactive and impulsive children. Others show success with imagery in the development of self-control programs [McBrien 1978].

One way that imagery can promote a relaxed state is by making short comparative statements to children such as, "Float like a feather," or, "Melt like ice." Stories such as those used with the stunt games can also be used with imagery. The adult reads the story and, with various degrees of adult guidance, children try to depict the activity in the reading selection by creating their own responses and helping themselves to relax. Following are examples.

The Growing Flowers

Flowers grow.
First they are seeds.
Be a seed.
Grow like a flower.
Keep growing.
Grow tall.
Now you are a flower.
Now wilt like a flower.

In this activity, a child acts out the growth of a flower. For the starting position, the child squats down low as close to the floor as possible, then stretches (grows) as tall as possible.

The adult can use a real flower or picture of a flower in the discussion about flowers, which can take into account the various kinds of flowers and what they need to make them grow and how they grow. Tension occurs during the growing period, and relaxation when the flower wilts.

Falling Leaves

Trees stand tall and straight.
Stand tall and straight like a tree.
Trees have leaves.
Leaves fall.
They fall from the trees.
They fall to the ground.
Fall like leaves.
Down, down, down.
Down to the ground.
Quiet leaves.
Rest like leaves.

This is an activity in which the child dramatizes leaves falling from a tree. The child stands straight and stiff like a tree and then does movements that depict falling leaves.

The adult can introduce the activity with any discussion about trees and their leaves. Tension occurs during the time the child stands stiff like a tree, and relaxation takes place as the child releases from the position and acts out the falling of leaves.

Mr. Snowman and Mr. Sun

See Mr. Snowman.
Mr. Snowman is packed
   with hard snow.
See Mr. Sun.
Mr. Sun is warm.
Mr. Snowman sees Mr. Sun.
Mr. Snowman is going.
Going, going, going.
Mr. Snowman is gone.
Be Mr. Snowman.

In this activity, the child dramatizes a melting snowman. In doing this, the child will give his or her idea of a snowman and what happens when the snowman melts.

There are many ways to introduce this activity. One of the most effective ways is to discuss the building of a snowman and how long it will take. The adult may lead a discussion on why a snowman melts. The child's body is tense as he or she becomes a snowman of hard-packed snow. Relaxation occurs when the child melts by being in the sun.

In closing this chapter, I would like to submit a word of caution. Although mental practice and imagery are sound techniques for helping children relax, it is possible that side effects might occur with certain children. For example, a borderline psychotic child could possibly be harmed by imagery activities.

It has been the purpose of this book to provide adults with some insights into the practice of helping children manage stress. The various activities for childhood stress management suggested in the book should be considered as representative examples of an almost unlimited number of possibilities. These activities have numerous possible variations that the discerning reader will notice immediately. Therefore, I heartily recommend that these activities be used as a point of departure for the development of other experiences for the management of childhood stress.

Notes

Koehler, G. (1987, November/December). Stress management for children. *Strategies*, 17

Luria, A. R. (1959). Development of the directive function of speech in early childhood. *Word*, 15.

McBrien, R. J. (1987, February). Using relaxation methods with first grade boys. *Elementary School Guidance and Counseling*, 87.

Suggestions for Further Reading

Austin, J. S. (1995). Prevent school failure: Treat test anxiety. *Preventing School Failure, 40*, 10-13.

Baldwin, S. (1994). All stressed out. *Scholastic Early Childhood Today, 9*, 22.

Beardsall, L. & Dunn, J. (1992). Adversities in childhood: Siblings' experiences and their relations to self-esteem. *Journal of Child Psychology and Psychiatry & Allied Disciplines, 33*, 349-359.

Beckman, P. J. (1991). Comparisons of mothers' and fathers' perceptions of the effect on young children with and without disabilities. *American Journal of Mental Retardation, 95*, 585-595.

Berden, G. (1990). Major life events and changes in behavioural functioning of children. *Journal of Child Psychology and Psychiatry & Allied Disciplines, 31*, 949-959.

Black, S. (1996). Helping depressed students. *The Education Digest, 62*, 53-56.

Butte, H. P. (1993). Developing curriculum to reduce emotional stress in middle schoolers. *Middle School Journal, 24*, 41-46.

Carson, D. K. (1992). Stress and coping as predictors of young children's development and psychosocial adjustment. *Child Study Journal, 22*, 273-302.

DeWolfe, A., & Saunders, A. M. (1995). Stress reduction in sixth-grade students. *The Journal of Experimental Education, 63*, 315-329.

Domenech, D. A. (1996). Surviving the ultimate stress. *School Administrator, 53,* 40-41.

Egeland, B., & Susman-Stillman, A. (1996). Dissociation as a mediator of child abuse across generations. *Child Abuse & Neglect, 20,* 1123-1132.

Ethier, L. S. (1995). Childhood adversity, parental stress, and depression of negligent mothers. *Child Abuse & Neglect, 19,* 19-32.

Fagan, D. B. (1996). Relationships between parent-child relational variables and child test variables in highly stressed urban families. *Child Study Journal, 26,* 87-108.

Famularo, R. (1996). Psychiatric comorbidity in childhood post traumatic stress disorder. *Child Abuse & Neglect, 20,* 953-961.

Filippelli, L. A., & Jason, L. (1992). How life events affect the academic adjustment and self-concept of transfer children. *Journal of Instructional Psychology, 19,* 61-65.

Fleege, P. O. (1992). Stress begins in kindergarten: A look at behavior during standardized testing. *Journal of Research in Childhood Education, 7,* 20-26.

Fredericks, A. D. (1990). Stress and your child. *Teaching PreK-8, 20,* 38.

Furman, R. A. (1995). Help kids cope with their feelings. *The Education Digest, 50,* 23-27.

Ghaziuddin, M. (1995). Life events and depression in children with pervasive developmental disorders. *Journal of Autism and Developmental Disorders, 25,* 495-502.

Goodman, G. S. (1991). Children's memory for stressful events. *Merrill-Palmer Quarterly, 37,* 109-157.

Goodyer, I. M. (1990). Recent life events and psychiatric disorder in school-age children. *Journal of Psychology and Psychiatry & Allied Disciplines, 31,* 839-848.

Hendesson, P. A. (1992). Effects of a stress-control program on children's locus of control, self-concept and coping behavior. *The School Counselor, 40,* 125-130.

Henniger, M. L. (1995). Play: Antidote for childhood stress. *Early Child Development and Care, 105,* 7-12.

Hobson, M. L. & Rejeski, W. J. (1993). Does the dose of acute exercise mediate psychophysiological responses to mental stress? *Journal of Sport and Exercise Psychology, 15,* 77-87.

Huber, J. D., & Garten, T. R. (1993). Causes, consequences, and reduction of distress and burnout among rural middle school students. *Rural Education, 14,* 11-13.

Hura, S. L., & Echols, C. H. (1996). The role of stress and articulatory difficulty in children's early production. *Developmental Psychology, 32,* 165-176.

Jean, R. E. (1995, Fall). Stress in families with chronically ill children. *Journal of Family and Consumer Sciences,* 47-52.

Jenkins, J. M., & Smith, M. A. (1990). Factors protecting children living in disharmonious homes: Maternal reports. *Journal of the American Academy of Child and Adolescent Psychiatry, 29,* 60-69.

Johnson, H. L. (1993). Stressful family experiences and young children: How the classroom teacher can help. *Intervention in School and Clinic, 28,* 165-171.

Katz, L. (1996). Helping kids cope with frustration at school. *Instructor, 106,* 95-98.

Kees, N. L., & Lashwood, J. (1996). Compassion fatigue and school personnel: Remaining open to the affective needs of children. *Educational Horizons, 75,* 41-44.

Killen, K. (1996): How far have we come in dealing with the emotional challenge of abuse and neglect? *Child Abuse & Neglect, 20,* 791-795.

Lamarine, R. J. (1995). Child and adolescent depression. *The Journal of School Health, 65,* 390-393.

Leischow, S. J., & Bigelow, G. E. (1994). Stress reactivity: A simple classroom demonstration. *Journal of Health Education, 25,* 101-102.

Mellins, C. A., (1996). Children's methods of coping with stress: A twin study of generic and environmental influences. *The Journal of Child Psychology and Psychiatory & Allied Disciplines, 37,* 721-730.

Omizo, M. M., & Omizo, S. A. (1990). Children and stress: Using a phenomenological approach. *Elementary School Guidance & Counseling, 25,* 30-36.

Plante, T. G. (1993). Are stress and coping associated with aptitude and achievement testing performance among children? A preliminary investigation. *Journal of School Psychology, 31,* 259-266.

Power, L. (1990). Strategies for managing the alarm reaction. *The Education Digest, 56,* 61-63.

Prentice, B. (1993). Coping with stress. *The Instramentalist, 47,* 37-38.

Rende, R. D., & Plomin, K. (1991). Child and parent perceptions of the upsettingness of major life events. *Journal of Child Psychology and Psychiatry & Allied Disciplines, 32,* 627-633.

Romano, J. L. (1996). Stress and well-being in the elementary school: A classroom curriculum. *Journal of Instructional Psychology, 43,* 268-276.

Rossman, B. B. R. (1992). School-age children's perceptions of coping with distress: Strategies for emotional regulation and the moderation of adjustment. *Journal of Child Psychology and Psychiatry & Allied Disciplines, 33,* 1373-1397.

Rossman, B. B. R., & Rosenberg, M. S. (1992). Family stress and functioning in children: The moderating effects of children's beliefs about their control over parental conflict. *Journal of Child Psychology and Psychiatry & Allied Disciplines, 33,* 699-715.

Sharrer, V. W., & Ryan-Wenger, N. M. (1991). Measurements of stress and coping among school-aged children with and without recurrent abdominal pains. *The Journal of School Health, 61,* 86-91.

Silvestri, L. (1996). The effects of a self development program and relaxation/imagery training on anxiety levels of at-risk fourth grade students. *Journal of Instructional Psychology, 23,* 167-173.

Simplicio, J. S. C. (1995). Can moderate physical activity reduce stress and improve examination scores. *Journal of Instructional Psychology, 22,* 64-76.

Wanko, M. A. (1995). Cut stress now. *The Education Digest, 60,* 40-41.

Watson, R. G. (1990). Take steps to prevent stress-produced burn-out. *School Shop Tech Directions, 50,* 37.

Whitebook, M. (1994). Give yourself a break: Reducing stress for child care workers. *Scholastic Early Childhood Today, 8,* 10-11.

About the Author

James H. Humphrey, Ed.D., Professor Emeritus at the University of Maryland, has authored or coauthored 47 books and edited 41 others. His 200 articles and research reports have been published in more than 20 different national and international journals and magazines. Considered a pioneer in stress education, he is the founder and editor of *Human Stress: Current Selected Research*. In the early 1980s, he collaborated with the late Hans Selye, who is generally known as the father of stress, on certain aspects of childhood stress research. Dr. Humphrey has received numerous educational honors and awards. He is a Fellow in the American Institute of Stress.